ALL THE BUILDINGS* IN MELBOURNE

*THAT I'VE DRAWN SO FAR
BY JAMES GULLIVER HANCOCK

INTRODUCTION
BY JAMES GULLIVER HANCOCK

My hometown, Sydney, is a little less than 900 kilometres (560 miles) from Melbourne, and in some ways is its complete opposite. Where Sydney sprawls and winds its way around hills and harbours, Melbourne is planned and gridded. Where Sydney is outdoor-oriented, with beaches taking priority in daily life, Melbourne is beautiful indoors, and the city welcomes visitors and locals alike with a host of cafés and cultural experiences. Whenever I visit, I'm pleasantly surprised by the differences between the two cities.

Melbourne was one of the first places that I travelled to as a young person, and where I was struck by the understanding that there could even *be* different cities. It's really not until you've made a place your home and then travelled to another that you realise that the world is bigger than you think—that there are infinite ways to live beyond what you're familiar with. This feeling of infinite existence first hit me in Melbourne, and meant that the city has always held a hallowed place in my travels. It was this initial shock that eventually sent me exploring the world to see all of the possible ways to live.

The architecture and the trams were the first things I noticed in Melbourne, as is the case for most visitors. Decoration adorns the buildings, with little, dripping gothic towers found on the most unlikely streets. With dense high-street traffic and fascinating shops jostling side by side, the city conjures up the impression of a European atmosphere; whenever I'm in Melbourne and I'm walking the streets, I feel like I'm in a scene from another place—and maybe another time. Walking the grid transports me to Manhattan, New York, as I duck into little bars to shelter from the cold. Or to a little European city, sidling down an old alleyway to find a hidden treasure and experience the unexpected. It is easy to be romantic in Melbourne, to put on a duffel coat and pretend you're James Dean.

I soon learnt that what you can see on the streets is the city's rich, gold-infused history, and that historical connection publicly on display was fascinating to me, particularly the way it mirrored the day-to-day brushes with history you have in older cities around the world. During the Victorian gold rush of the 1850s, Melbourne was transformed into one of the world's largest and wealthiest cities, and you can see it! It feels like the whole city should be heritage-listed. I've always had interesting interactions with the architecture on my visits, whether it was exploring a friend's warehouse space secreted away behind the most wonderful facade and converted from a cavernous space into a rabbit warren of rooms; walking past fine diners under old chandeliers to get to a dark little whisky bar; or ducking out of the freezing cold into an old Victorian terrace house where you can eat the best noodles you've ever tasted. It seems common in Melbourne to juxtapose and reuse space, which is what makes it a fascinating and rewarding city to play with and discover.

I mostly seem to find myself in the inner north-east of the city, so that is where I started this adventure, drawing all the fun shops and churches and houses tucked away in unassuming streets. As I found myself falling in love with the place, I'd sometimes make up little stories about the daily life I would have if I lived in Melbourne. This process, which I also practised while drawing for *All the Buildings in New York*, allowed me to overcome my envy of a place, my desire to fill up my past with experiences of it. By sitting and drawing, my wanderings became conscious efforts to understand and make this lovely new place my own, as though I were inventing memories, substituting a tourist's passing love for a local's grounded experience.

Melbourne has always been a city I wander in; it's the perfect place to meander. And as I've mentioned in my other city books, it's these twisting journeys from place to place—sometimes with direction and sometimes without—that help me find the undiscovered gems, that see me turning a corner and running into a famous building or a derelict masterpiece. These discoveries are so exciting that the only way I can make myself take in the moment is to stop and draw. I'm a great believer in the power of drawing to make you perceive your surroundings with much greater intensity than if you were to just glance at them or even take a photo. Photography is brilliant, and I do use it for saving things to draw later when I don't have time, but you cannot beat the act of sitting in front of the thing you are drawing and sharing a moment with it. It's amazing what emerges when you stop and really look. And buildings are perfect for this exercise, because they don't move! Also, most of the time, buildings mark a significant place in the day-to-day life of the person drawing: they are part of a journey, and that is what I find really special. I treat my drawing like a diary, but instead of writing down sentences, I draw the things around me: buildings, the objects on a side table, or the things in my backpack. I love these drawings; when I stumble on an old one I am flooded with the memories of the moment in which I did that drawing. There might be an inkblot from when I got bumped by a passer-by; there might be a long-lost pair of glasses that I sat on days after I drew it, or a new pair of shoes that I bought that day. It's like a highly personal little map of a moment that pulls together literal objects, ephemeral accidents and coincidences with jottings of text.

I love the freedom of drawing like this: there are no mistakes, no clients and no end product, so I tend not to get too precious about my materials, pulling out whatever piece of scrap paper and ratty old pen that I might have on me to capture the moment, lending their quirks to the drawing. It's wonderful being on the move and drawing and not having access to all the comfortable crutches you can find in a studio or at home. You can't rely on the perfect cup of tea and the right music and the obsessively sharpened pencil; you just have to go at it with a ratty old felt-tip pen and a really absorbent piece of a napkin from lunch. As a consequence, you'll be surprised by lovely accidental experiments, things that you'll remember from a moment past.

As is the case with my other architecture books, I've tried to capture the city as a whole—it's not just postcards and vistas, but a very colloquial insider's look at the place. So, while I've included many of the famous buildings that are synonymous with Melbourne, I've also pulled in lots of personal and quirky places spread all around the city. As a result, you will find my friends' houses and my favourite gallery or café alongside the NGV and the Eureka Tower, or a granny's house on a side street right next to the MCG and the Arts Centre.

It's important to note that all the buildings in this book were built after European settlement in Australia. This part of Victoria was occupied by Indigenous Australians for 31,000 to 40,000 years before the arrival of Europeans. The Wurundjeri, Bunurong and Wathaurung peoples inhabited the area, which was an important meeting place for the five tribes of the Kulin nation alliance. I would like to acknowledge these people, who are the traditional custodians of this land. I would also like to pay respect to the elders, past and present, of the Kulin nation.

I hope you enjoy this personal exploration of Melbourne, and are encouraged to wander and start your own drawing journey, or follow along at www.allthebuildingsinmelbourne.com.

SOUTHBANK

PRINCES BRIDGE
BUILT IN 1888

BUILT ON THE SITE OF ONE OF THE OLDEST RIVER CROSSINGS IN AUSTRALIA

ACCA
AUSTRALIAN CENTRE FOR CONTEMPORARY ART

111 STURT ST.

DESIGNED BY WOOD MARSH ARCHITECTS COMPLETED IN 2002

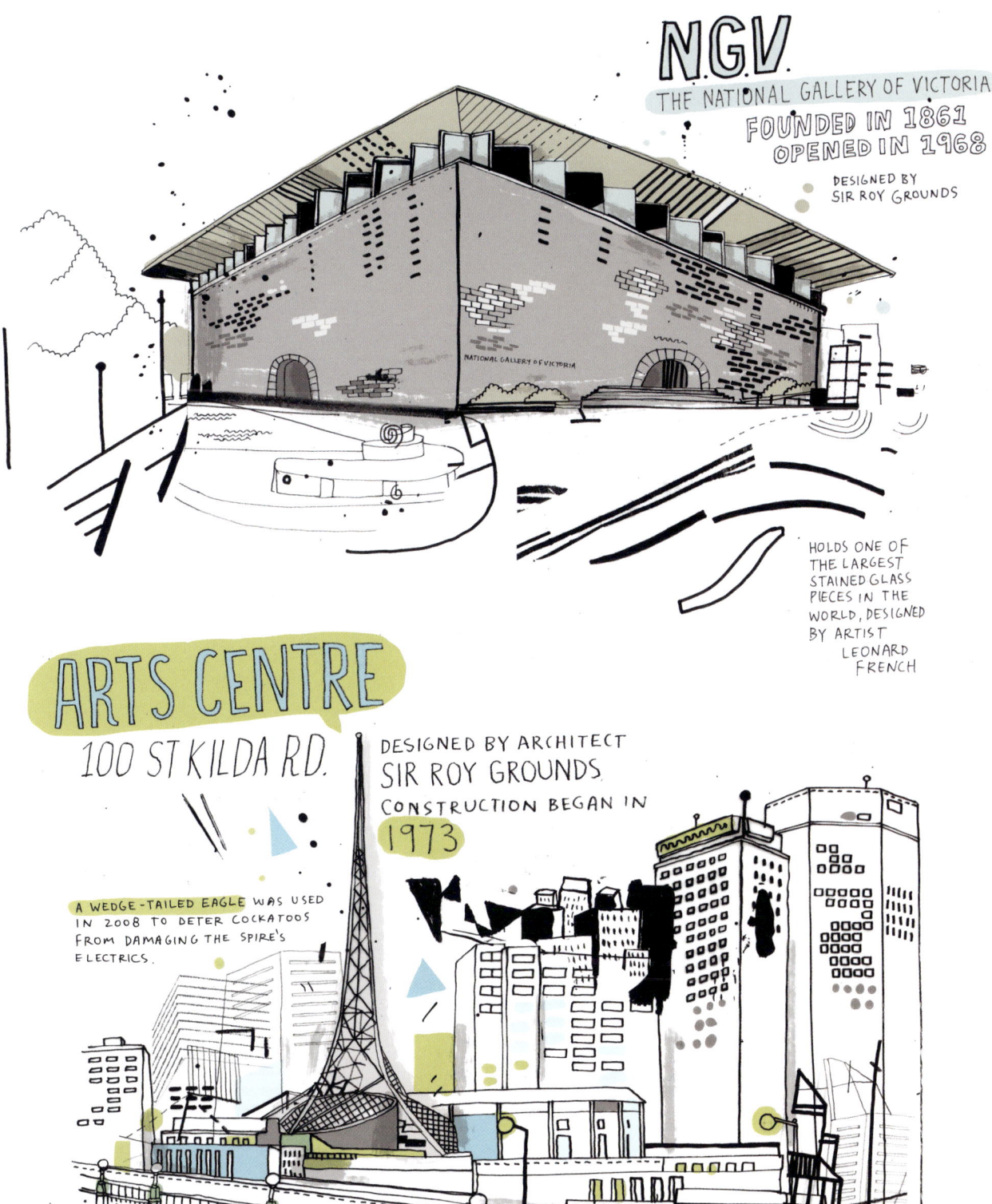

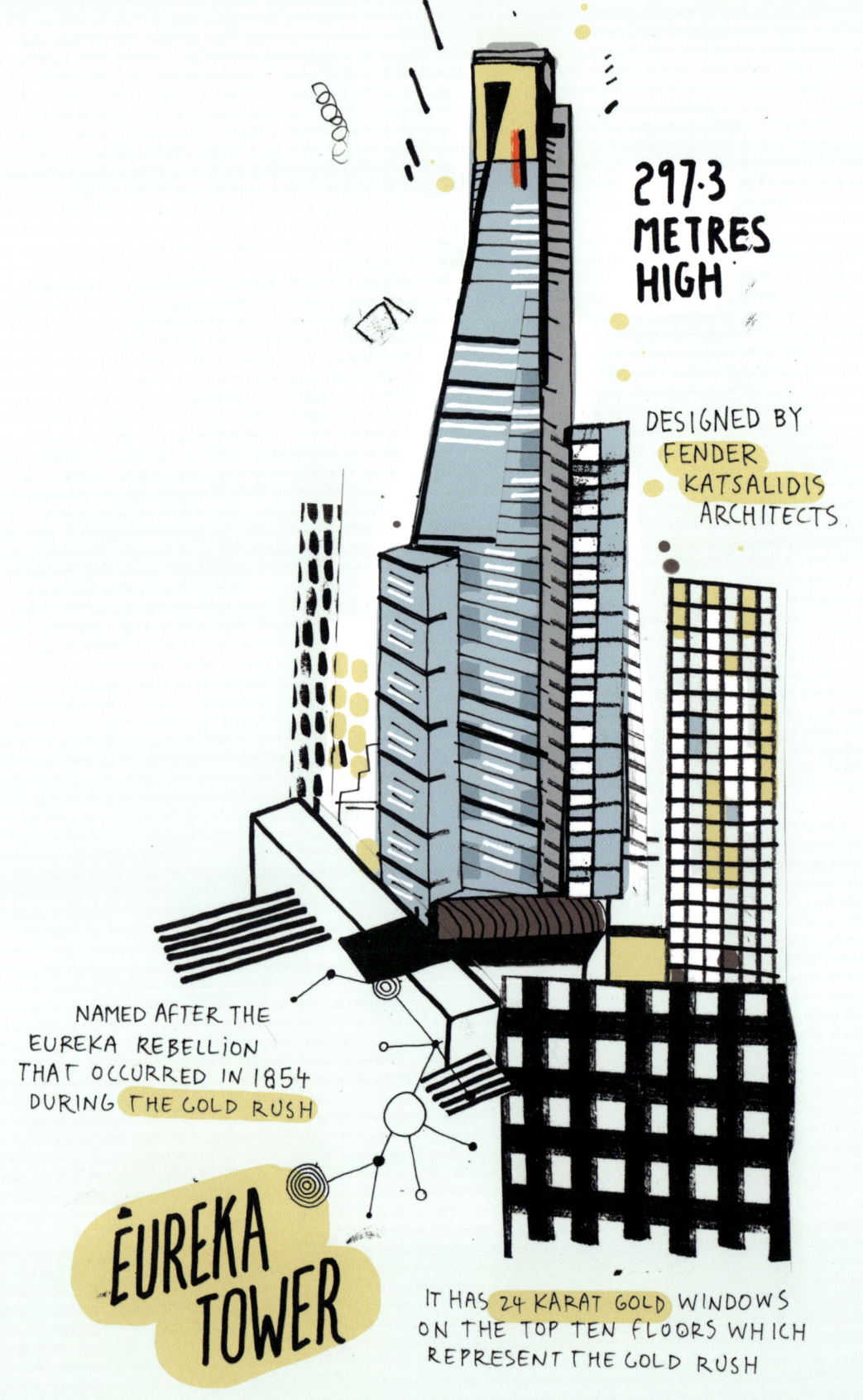

MELBOURNE CITY

FLINDERS STREET STATION

COMPLETED IN 1909 TO A FRENCH RENAISSANCE DESIGN BY RAILWAY EMPLOYEES JAMES FAWCETT & HPC ASHWORTH

THE FIRST RAILWAY STATION IN AN AUSTRALIAN CITY AVERAGES AROUND 90,000 VISITORS PER DAY!

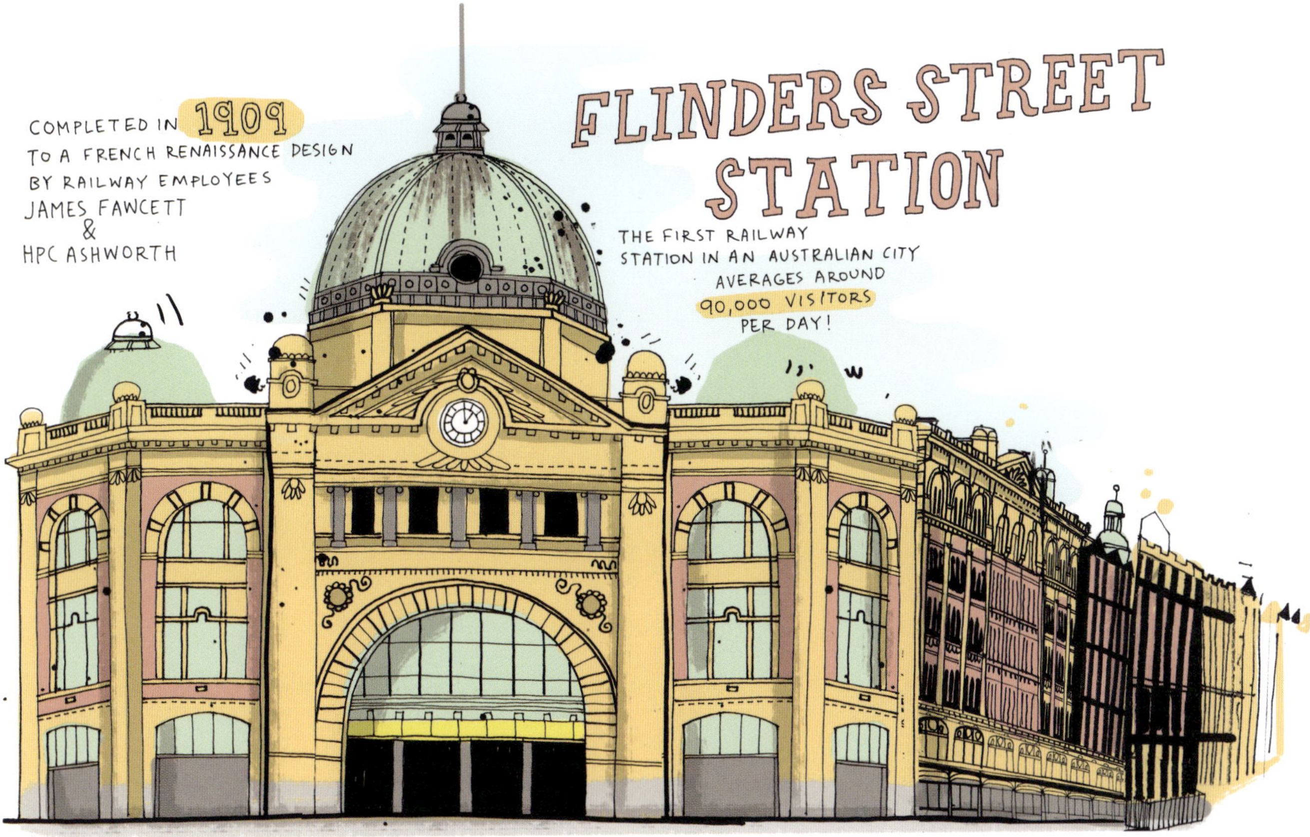

FEDERATION SQUARE

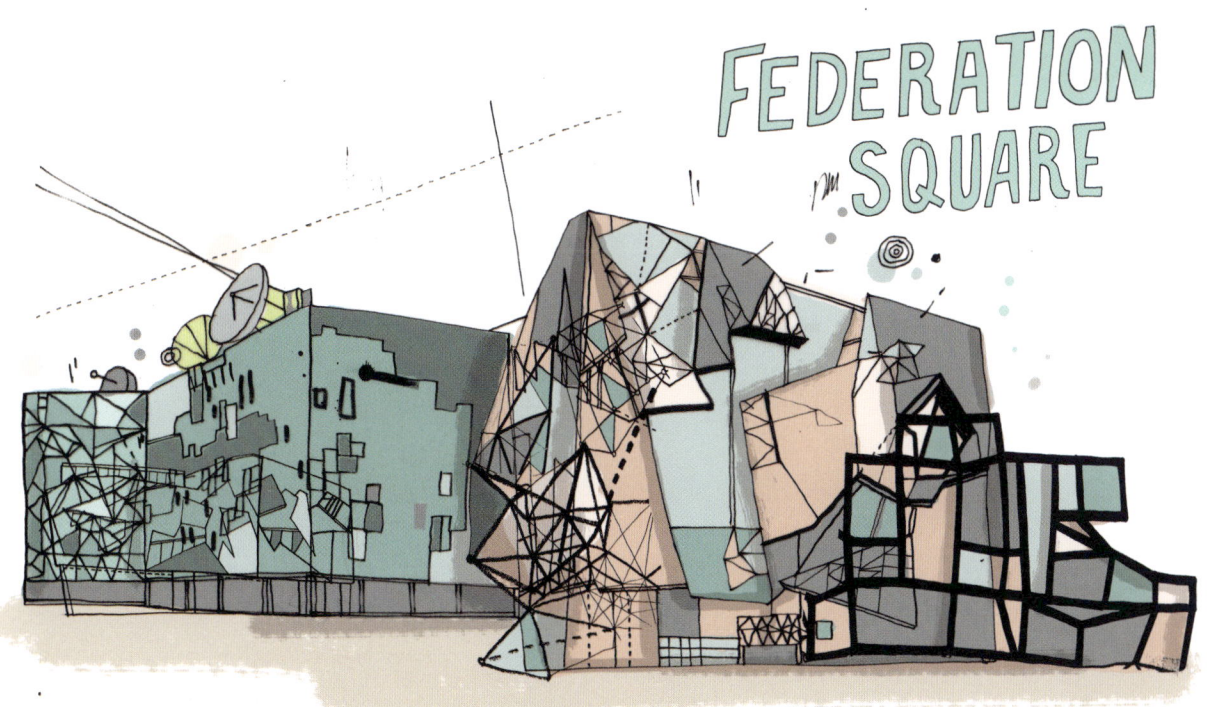

ST PAUL'S CATHEDRAL

MARKS THE PLACE OF THE FIRST CHRISTIAN SERVICE HELD IN MELBOURNE IN 1835

WILLIAM BUTTERFIELD DESIGNED THE CATHEDRAL IN THE GOTHIC TRANSITIONAL STYLE. THE FIRST BLOCK OF SANDSTONE WAS LAID IN 1880.

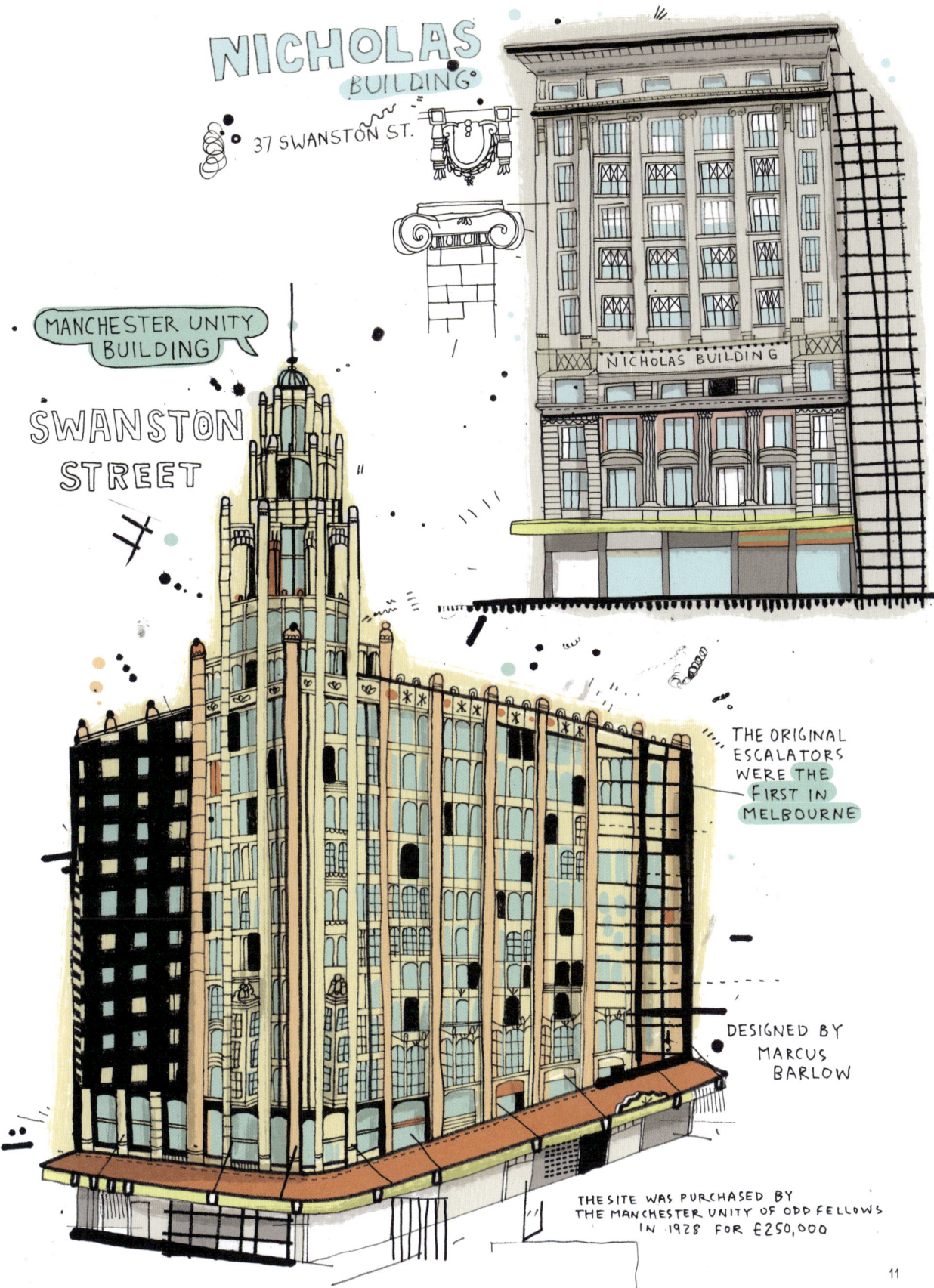

COLLINS ST.

THE IMMIGRATION MUSEUM

HOUSED IN THE OLD CUSTOMS HOUSE

162 COLLINS STREET

GPO
GENERAL POST OFFICE BUILDING
CNR. ELIZABETH ST. & BOURKE ST.

BUILT OVER **48 YEARS**!
THE CLOCKTOWER IS STILL USED TO MEASURE DISTANCES FROM MELBOURNE

CARLTON HOTEL
193 BOURKE ST.

66 BOURKE ST.

82-88
BOURKE
ST
AHSPENCER
HILL OF CONTENT
HILL OF CONTENT

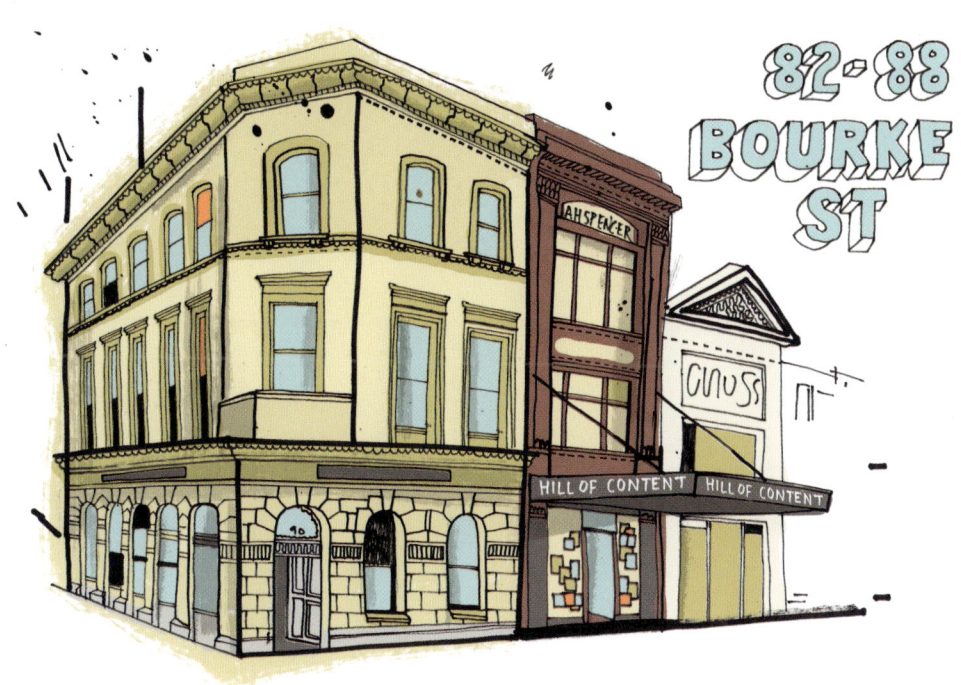

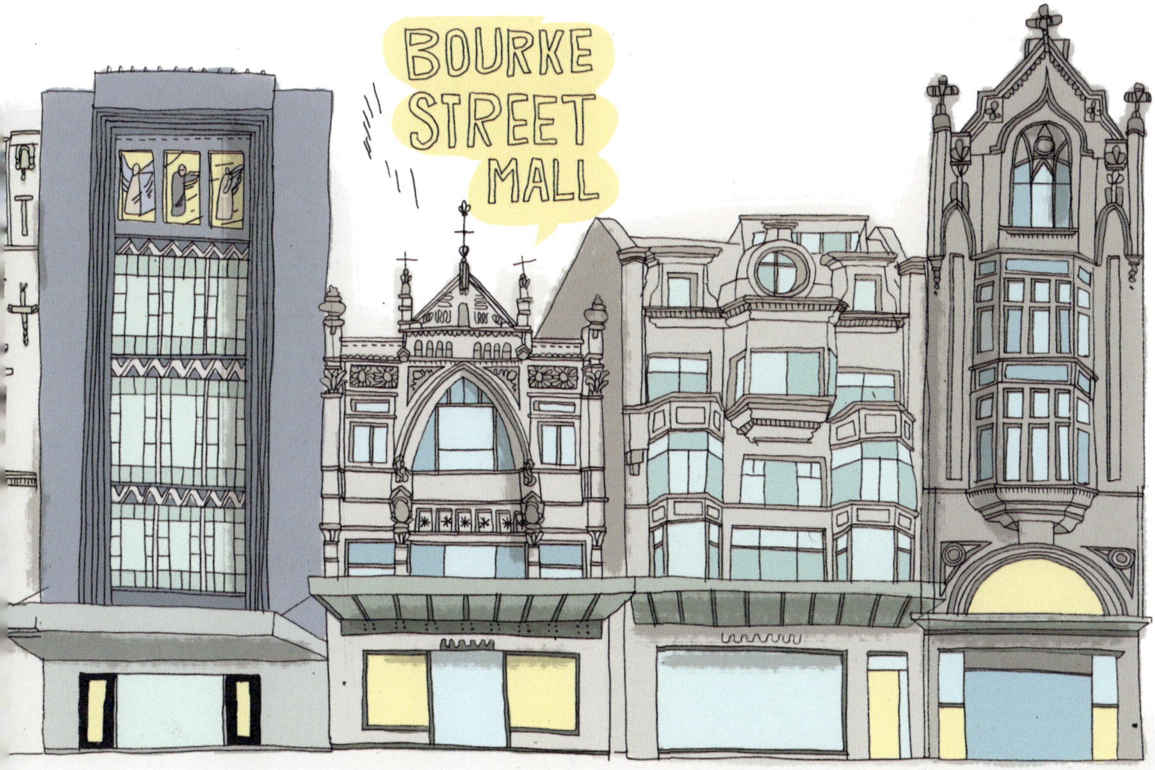
BOURKE
STREET
MALL

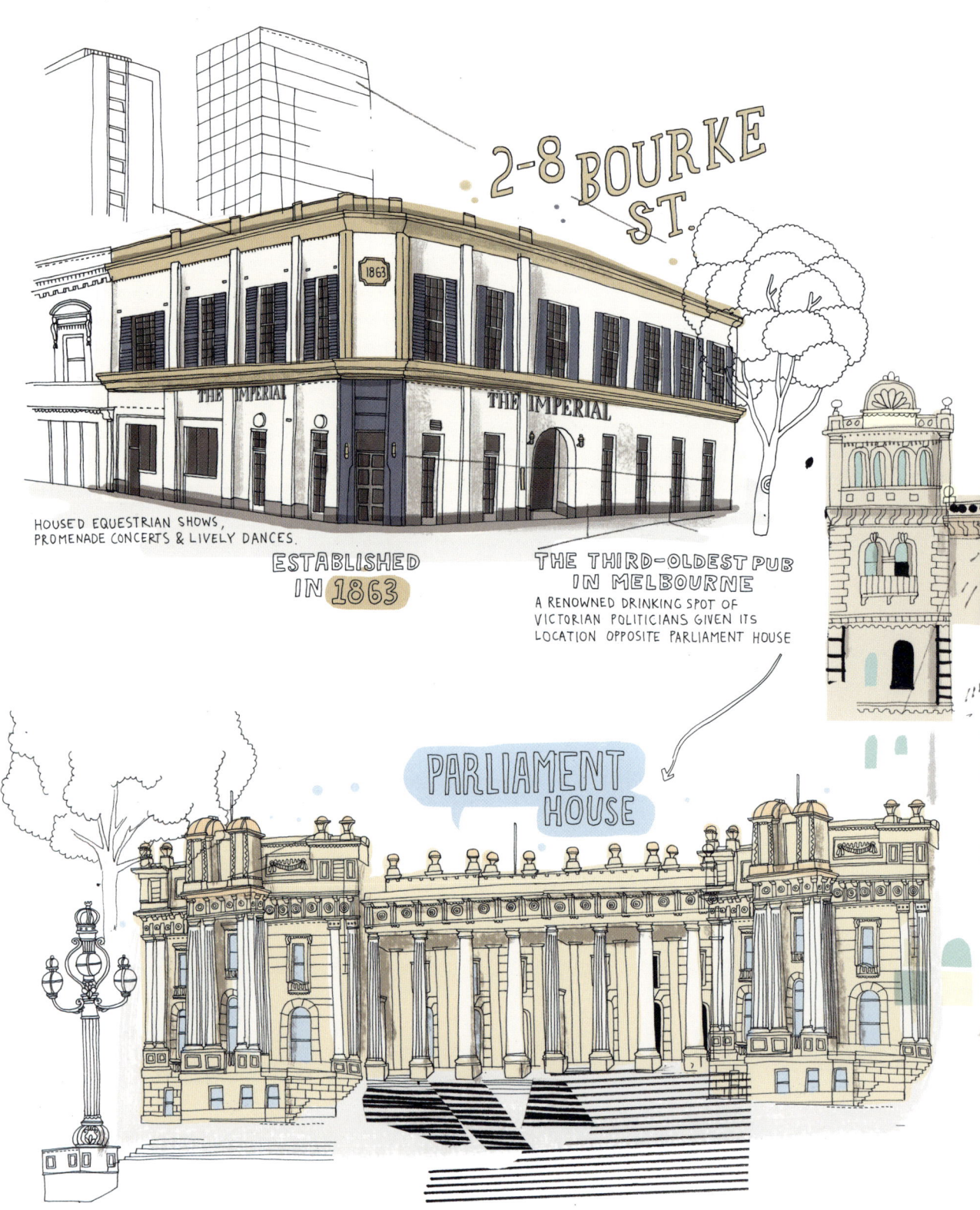

180 RUSSELL ST.

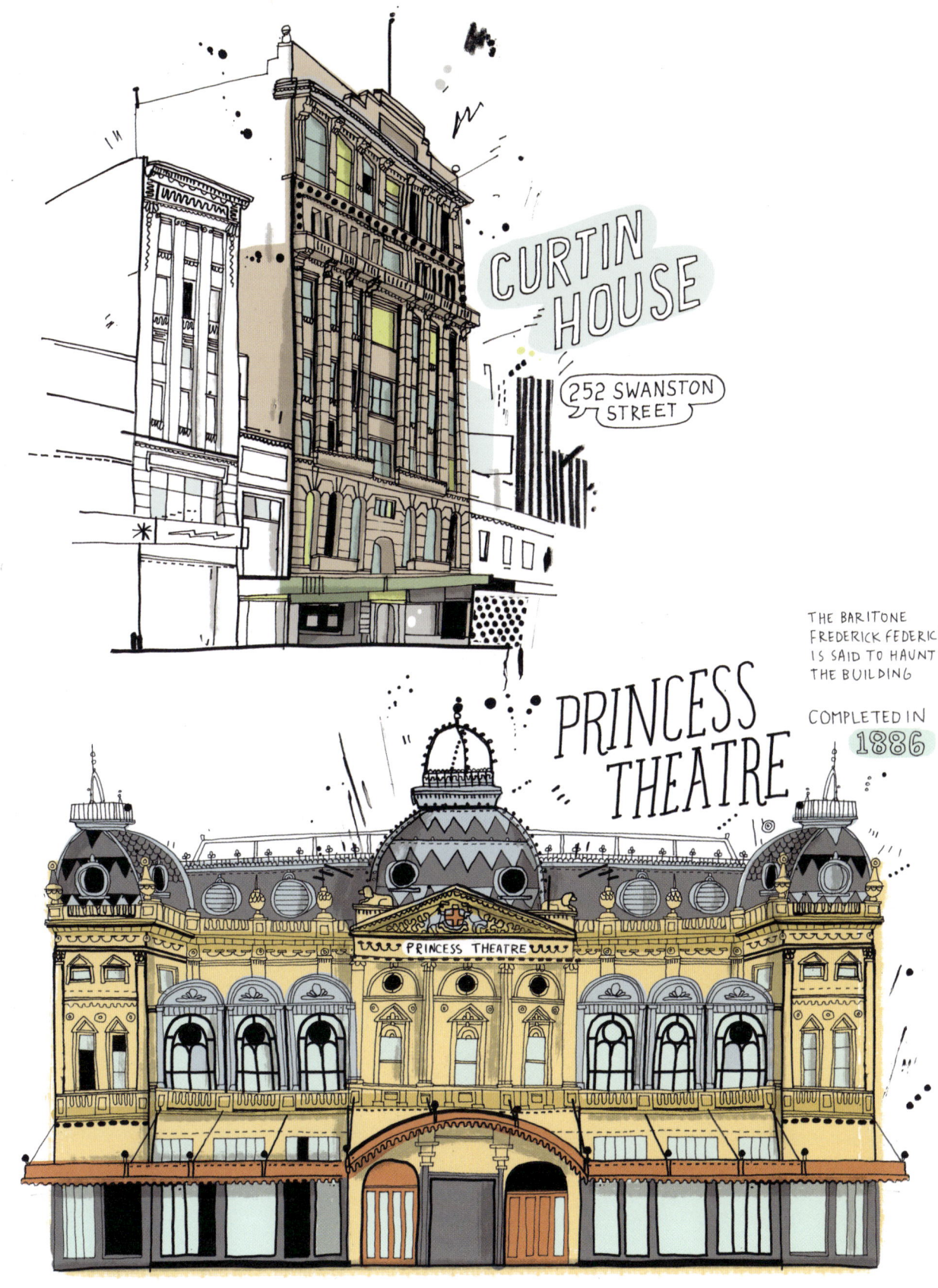

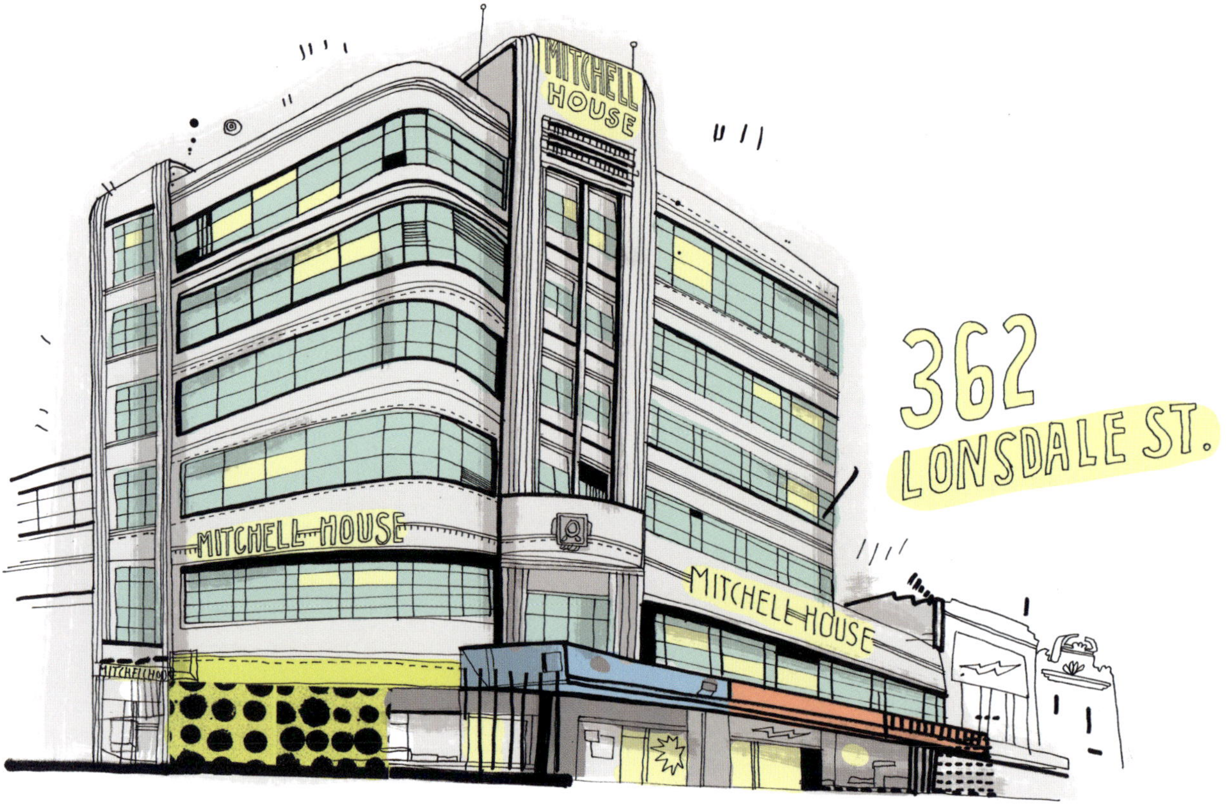

EMPORIUM
287 LONSDALE ST.

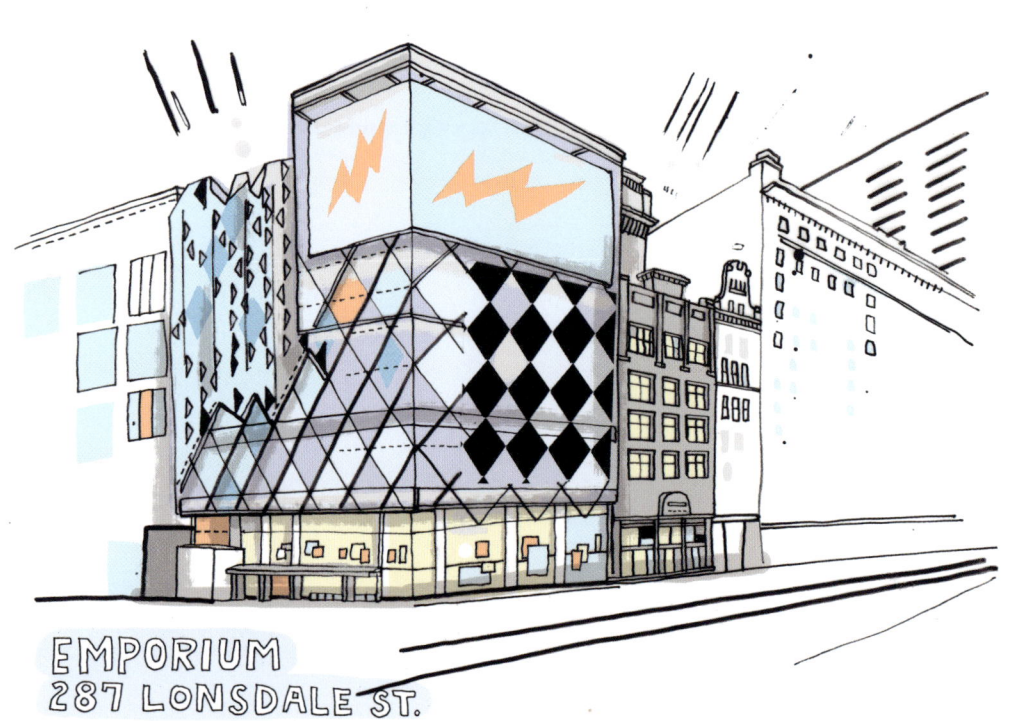

QUEEN VICTORIA MARKET
AKA 'VIC MARKET'

AT AROUND 17 ACRES IT IS THE LARGEST MARKET IN THE SOUTHERN HEMISPHERE

342-344 SWANSTON ST.

STOREY HALL

SWANSTON ACADEMIC BUILDING (BUILDING 80)
445 SWANSTON ST.

EAST MELBOURNE

THE OLD TREASURY

BUILT DURING THE GOLD RUSH TO HOUSE THE STATE'S GOLD
CONSTRUCTED BETWEEN 1858-62

DESIGNED BY 19-YEAR-OLD J.J. CLARK IN THE RENAISSANCE REVIVAL STYLE

CAPTAIN COOK'S COTTAGE

Y BATHS

BUILT IN 1860 TO STOP PEOPLE BATHING IN THE YARRA. THE CURRENT BUILDING WAS DESIGNED BY JOHN JAMES CLARK & OPENED IN 1904

CONSTRUCTED IN 1755 IN THE ENGLISH VILLAGE OF GREAT AYTON BY THE PARENTS OF CAPTAIN JAMES COOK

IT WAS DECONSTRUCTED BRICK BY BRICK AND PACKED IN 253 CASES AND 40 BARRELS AND SHIPPED TO AUSTRALIA ALONG WITH CUTTINGS OF THE VINES ON THE ORIGINAL HOUSE

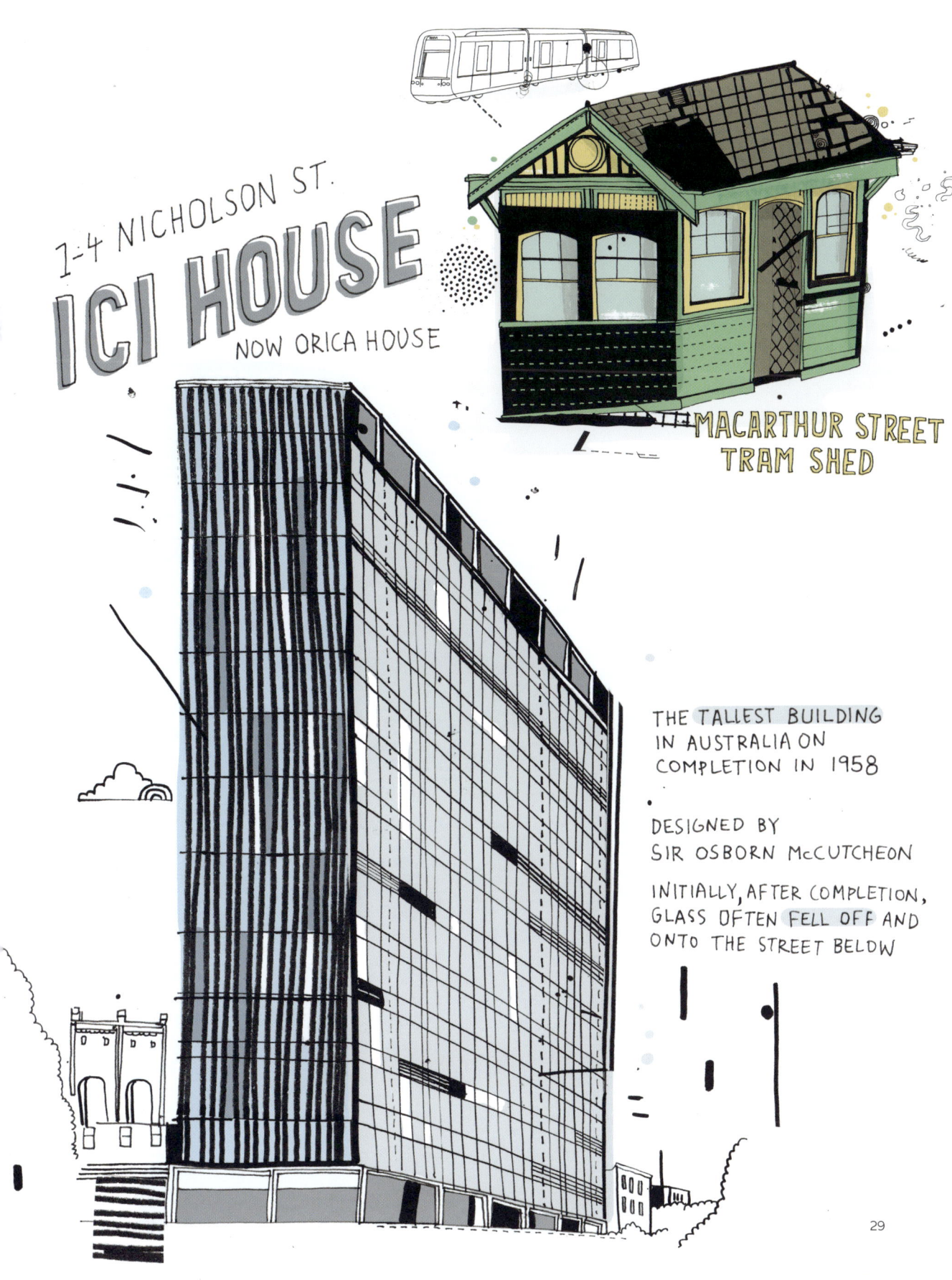

DOCKLANDS

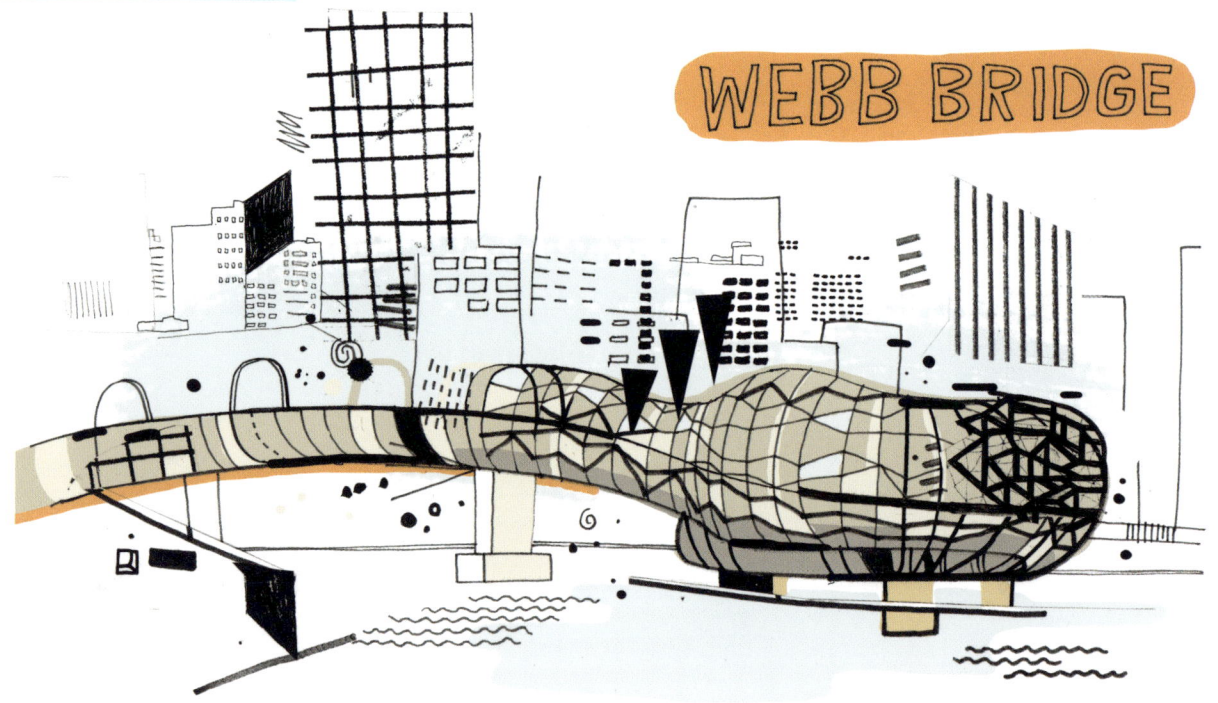

WEBB BRIDGE

60-78 GLEN EIRA RD.

ELSTERNWICK

RIPPON LEA ESTATE
BUILT IN 1868 FOR
SIR FREDERICK SARGOOD

RIPPONLEA

ST KILDA

LUNA PARK

THE FIRST OF FIVE LUNA PARKS BUILT IN AUSTRALIA
OPENED IN 1912
IT WAS BUILT BY THE AMERICAN PHILLIPS BROTHERS

THE ESPLANADE HOTEL

11 UPPER ESPLANADE
BUILT IN 1878

AKA 'THE ESPY'

ORIGINALLY BUILT AS THREE TERRACE HOUSES, BUT CHANGED DURING CONSTRUCTION

PALAIS THEATRE

CAULFIELD NORTH

LABASSA
2 MANOR GROVE

MALVERN

39-45 STATION ST.

by Rocco · ROCCO · 45 DENTAL SURGERY

PRAHRAN

282 CHAPEL ST.

CHEAPEST PRICES   BIGGEST RANGE

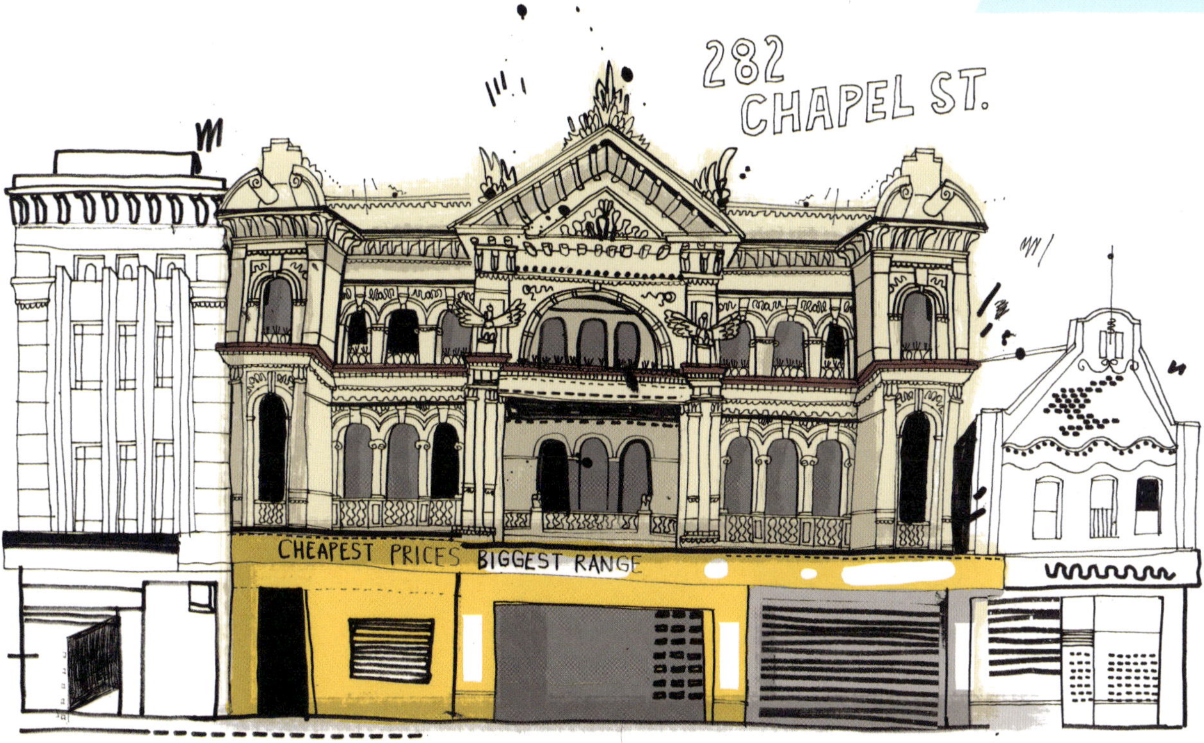

321-323 CHAPEL ST.

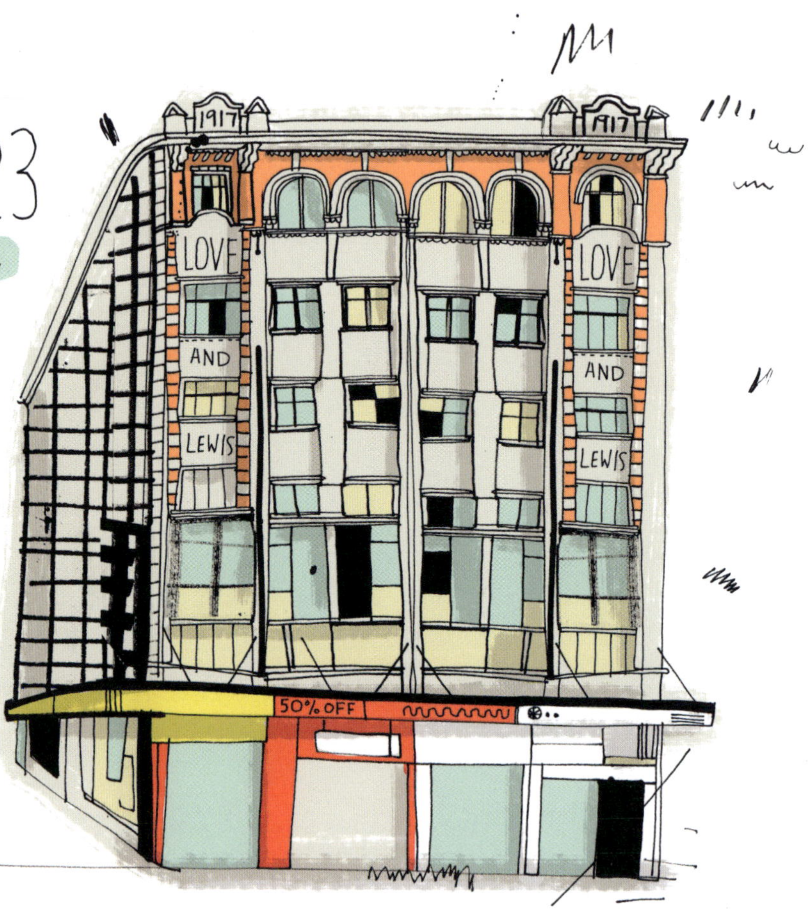
1917
1917
LOVE AND LEWIS
LOVE AND LEWIS
50% OFF

PRAHRAN MARKET

163 COMMERCIAL RD.

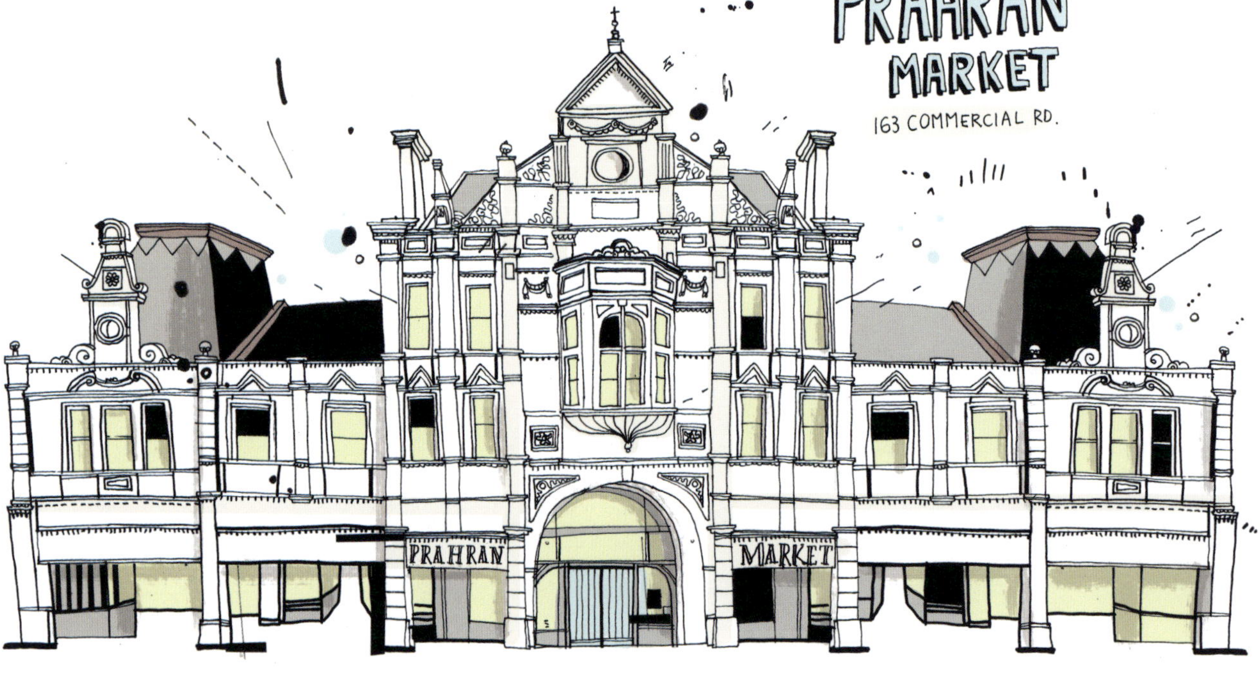
PRAHRAN
MARKET

VERMONT SOUTH

#2 PIN OAK COURT AKA **11 RAMSEY STREET** FROM NEIGHBOURS!

ALBERT PARK

160 BRIDPORT ST.

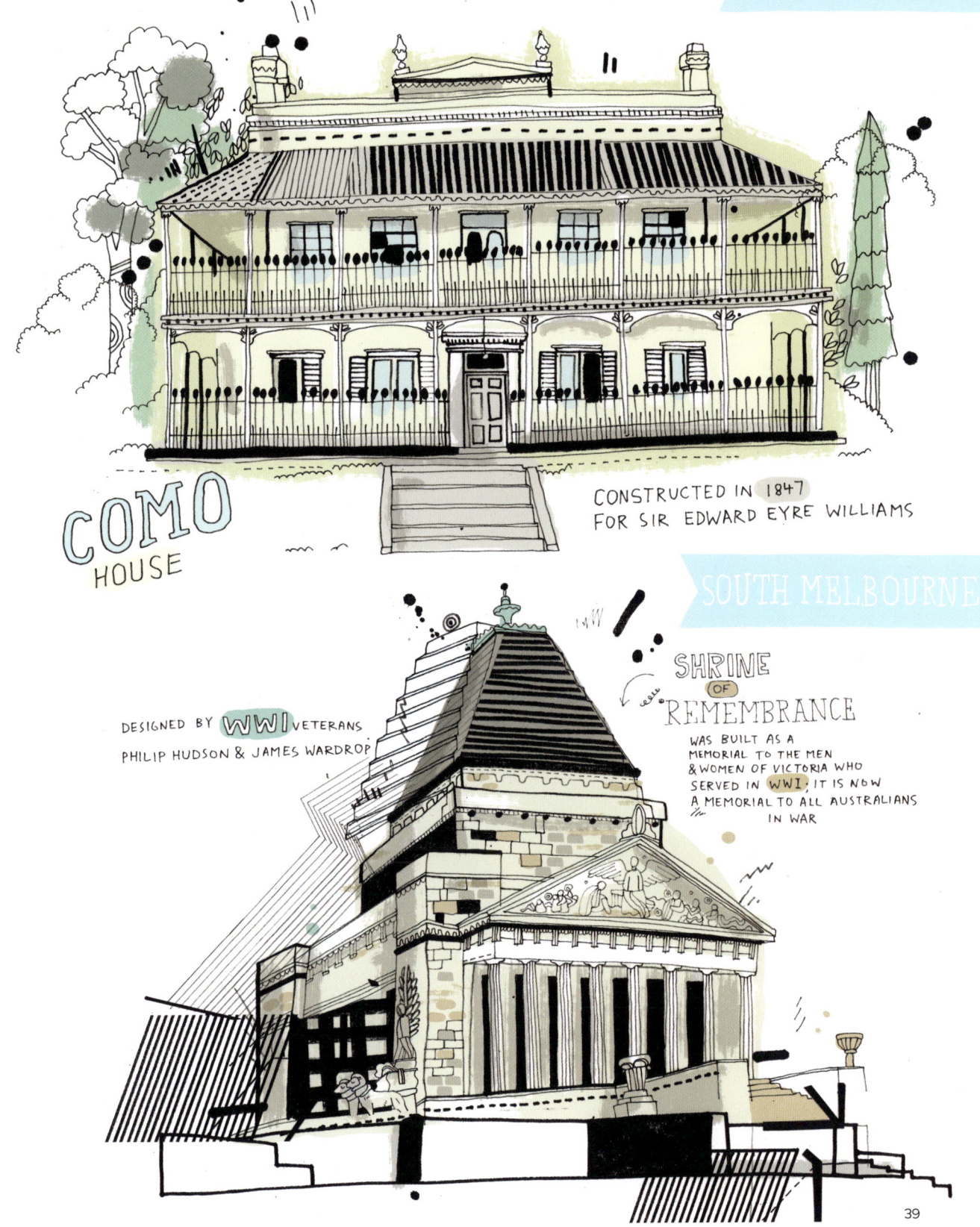

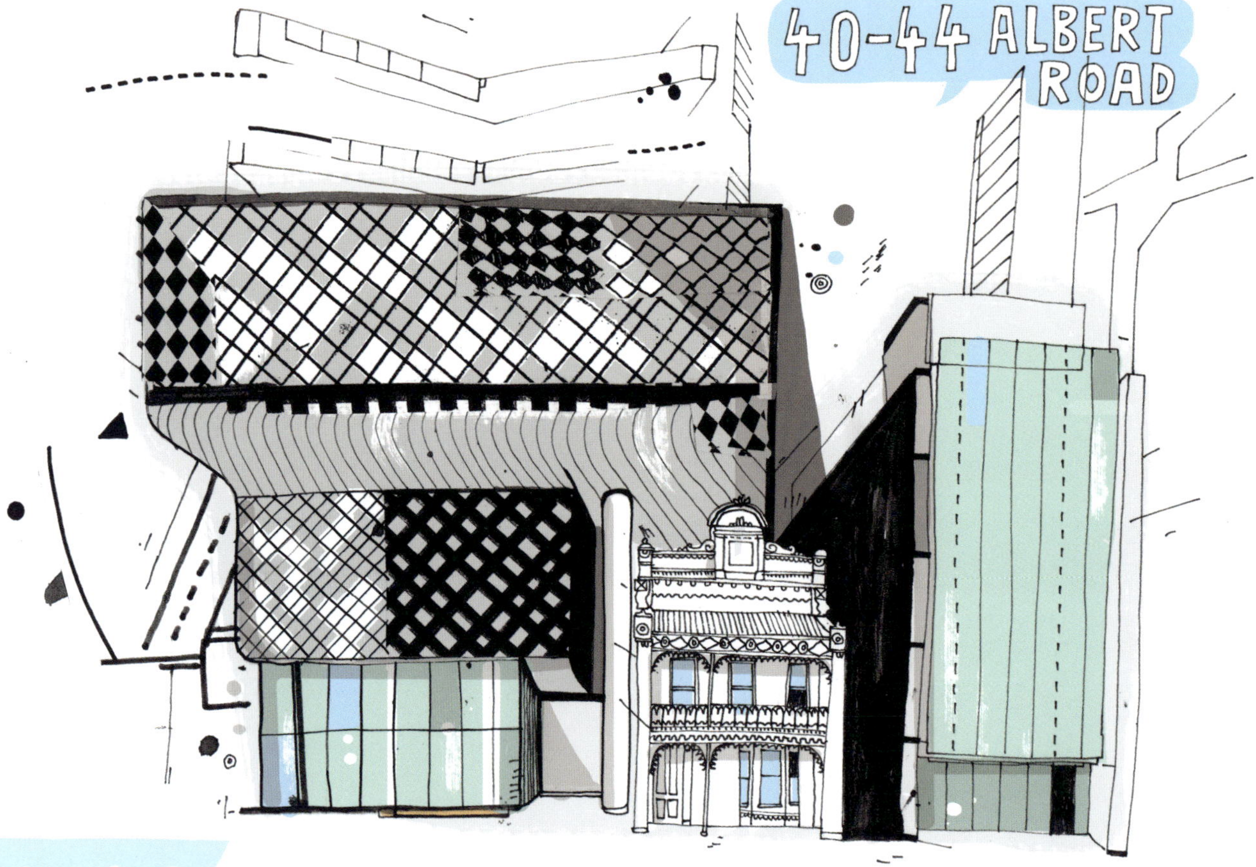
40-44 ALBERT ROAD

RICHMOND

PRINCE ALFRED
↳ NAMED AFTER QUEEN VICTORIA'S FOURTH CHILD.
619 CHURCH ST. RICHMOND
BUILT IN THE BAROQUE REVIVAL STYLE
PRINCE ALFRED HOTEL
619
BUILT IN 1893

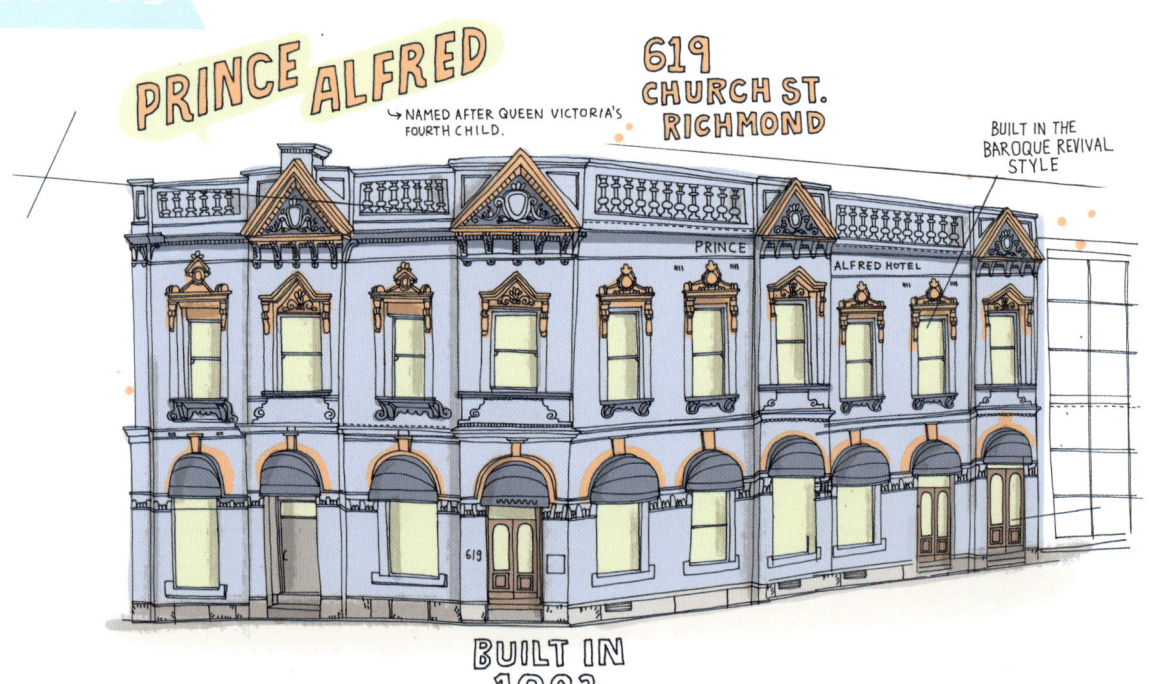

MELBOURNE RECTANGULAR STADIUM
AKA AAMI PARK

COMPLETED IN 2010
CAN SEAT UP TO 20,000–25,000 PEOPLE
DESIGNED BY COX ARCHITECTS

MELBOURNE CRICKET GROUND
MCG

THE LARGEST STADIUM IN AUSTRALIA

138-148 BRIDGE RD.

KEW

THE MCINTYRE HOUSE

2 HODGSON STREET

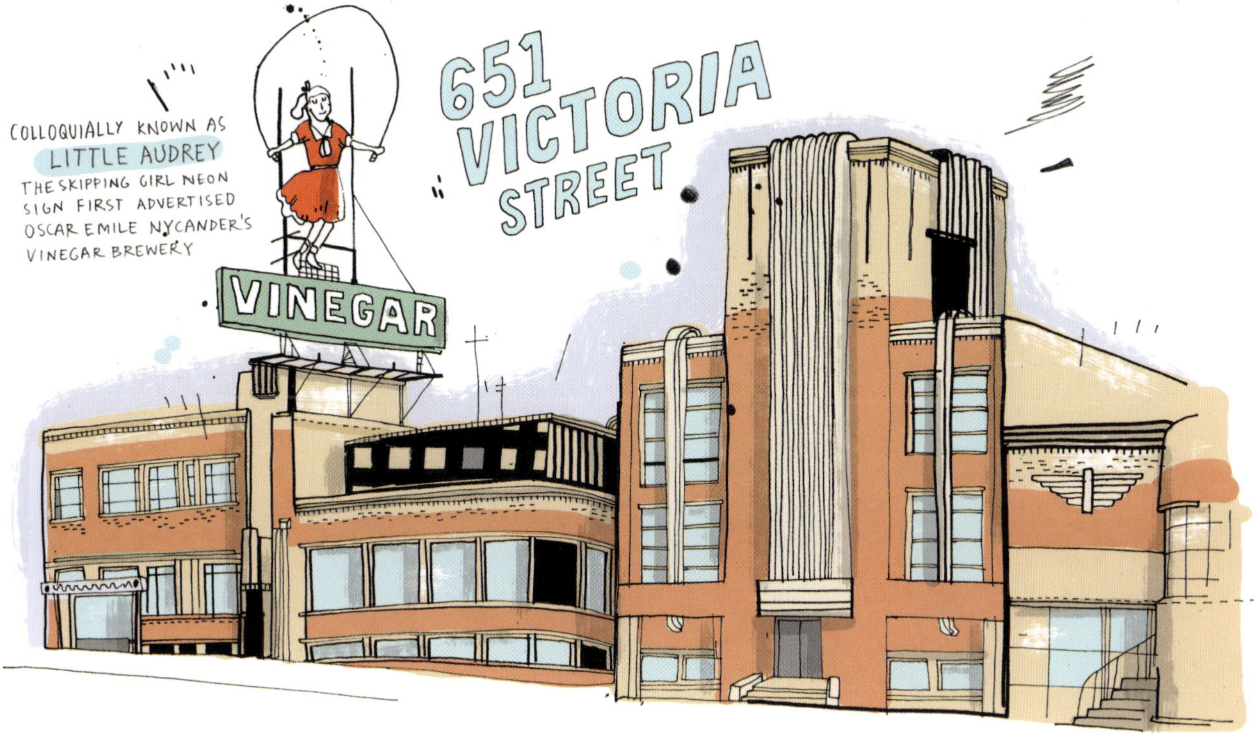
651 VICTORIA STREET
COLLOQUIALLY KNOWN AS
LITTLE AUDREY
THE SKIPPING GIRL NEON SIGN FIRST ADVERTISED OSCAR EMILE NYCANDER'S VINEGAR BREWERY
VINEGAR

35 PARK ST.

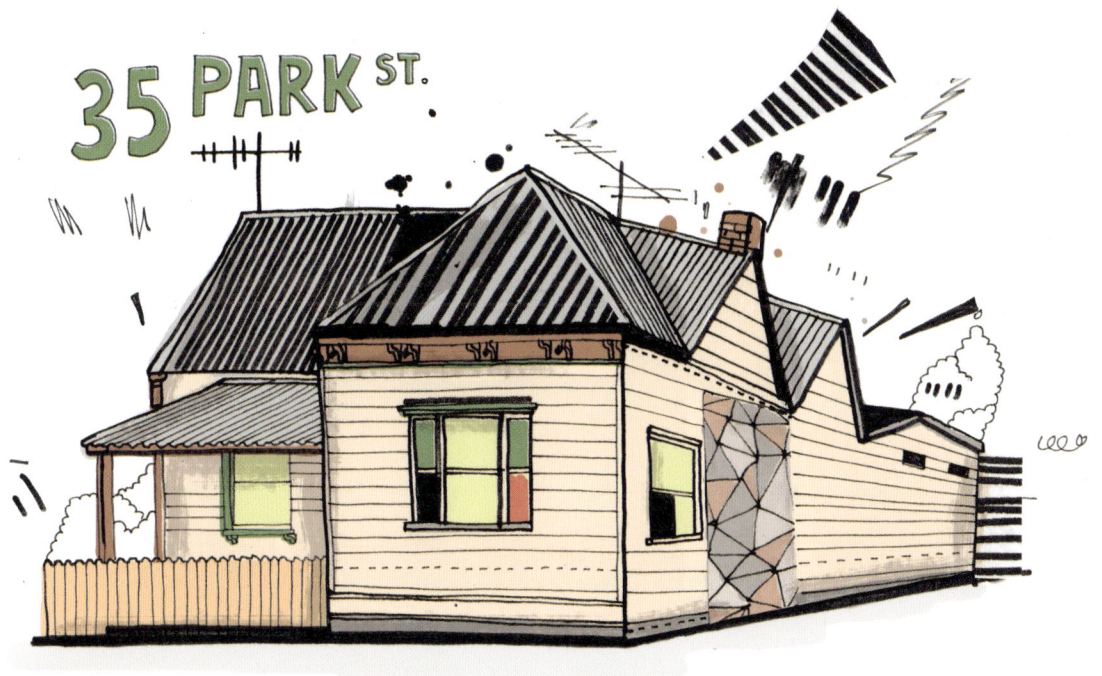

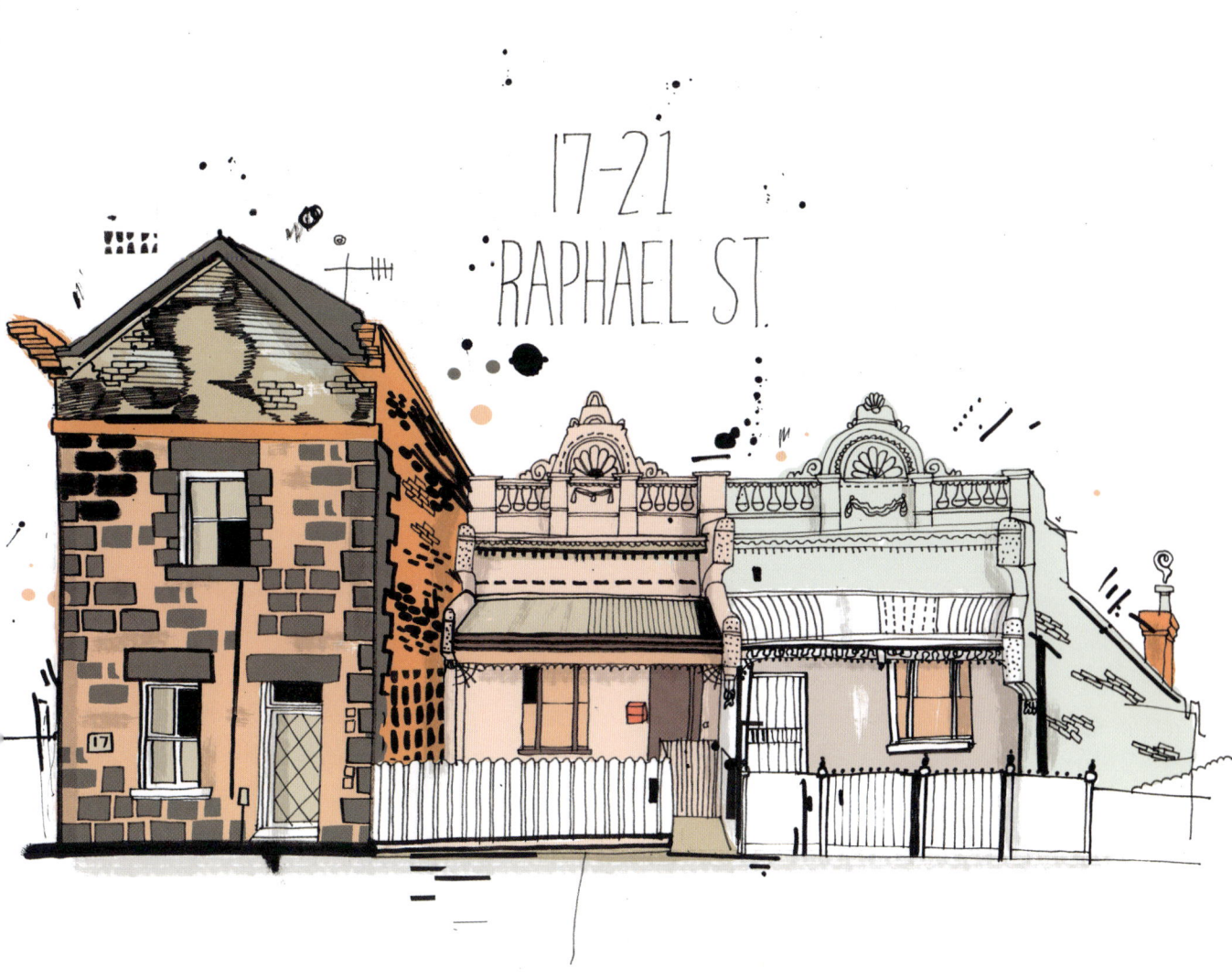

99-105 SACKVILLE ST

CLIFTON HILL

199 QUEENS PARADE

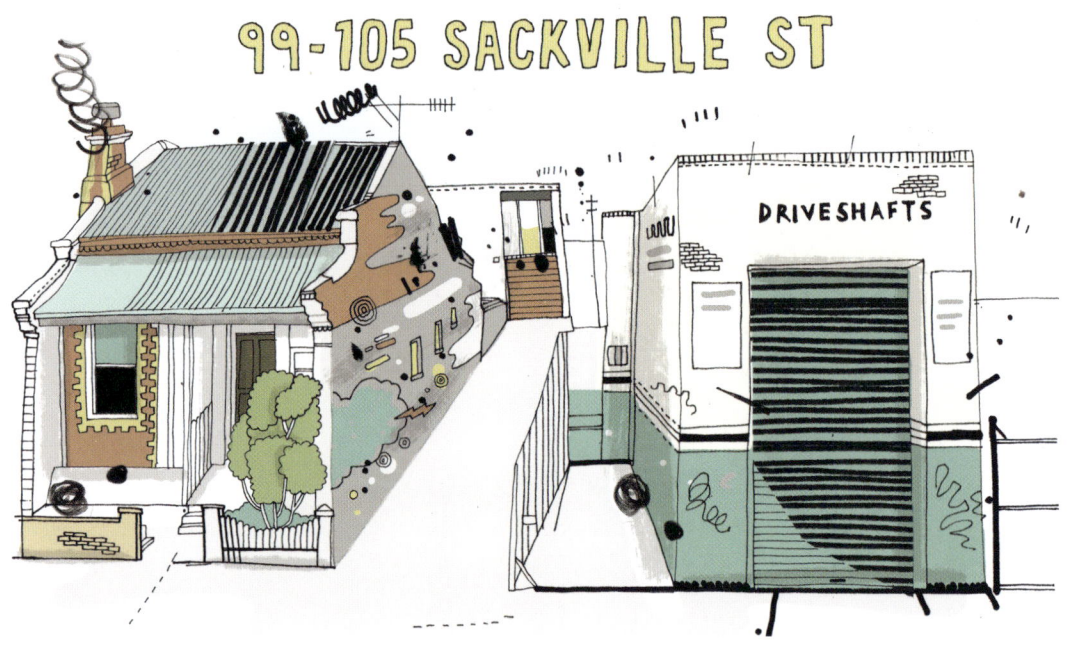

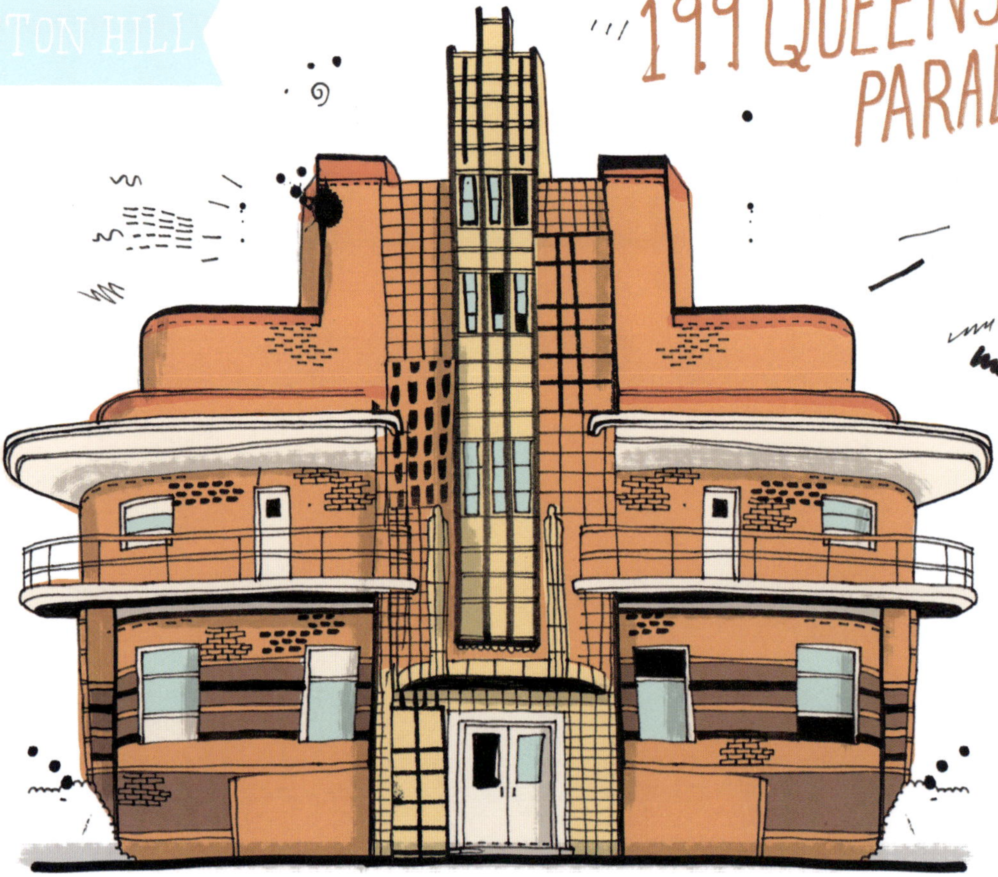

93-99 GEORGE ST

90 BRUNSWICK ST

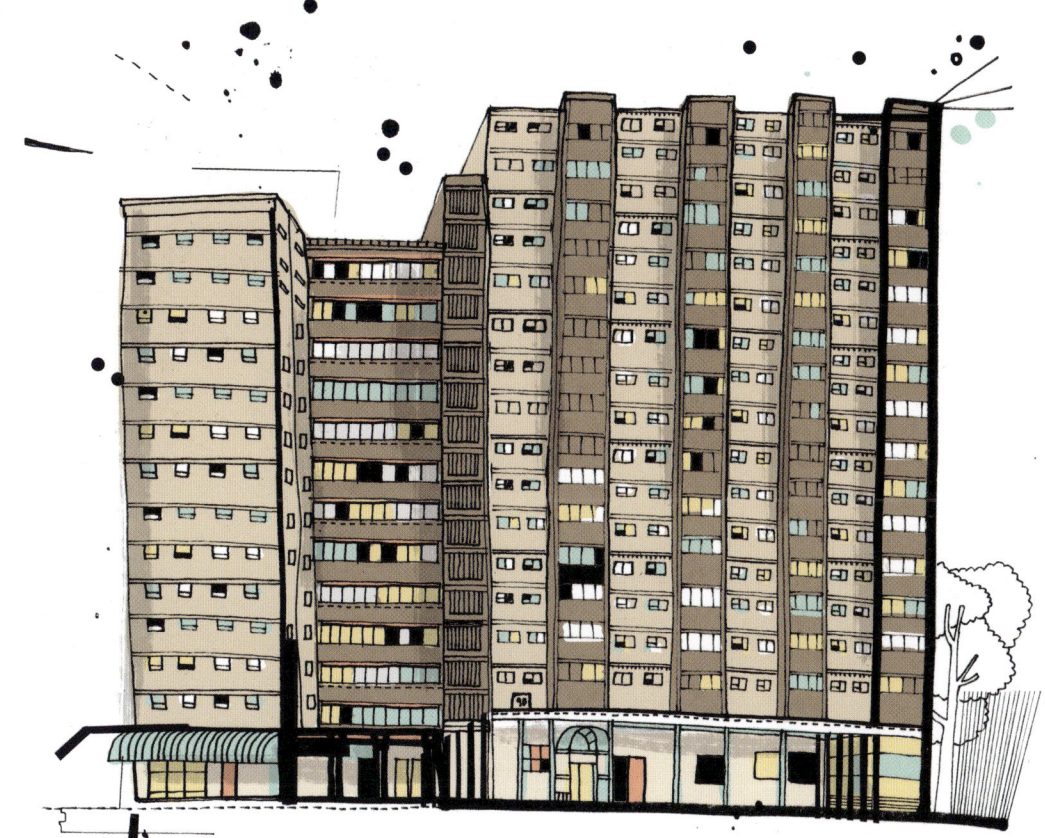

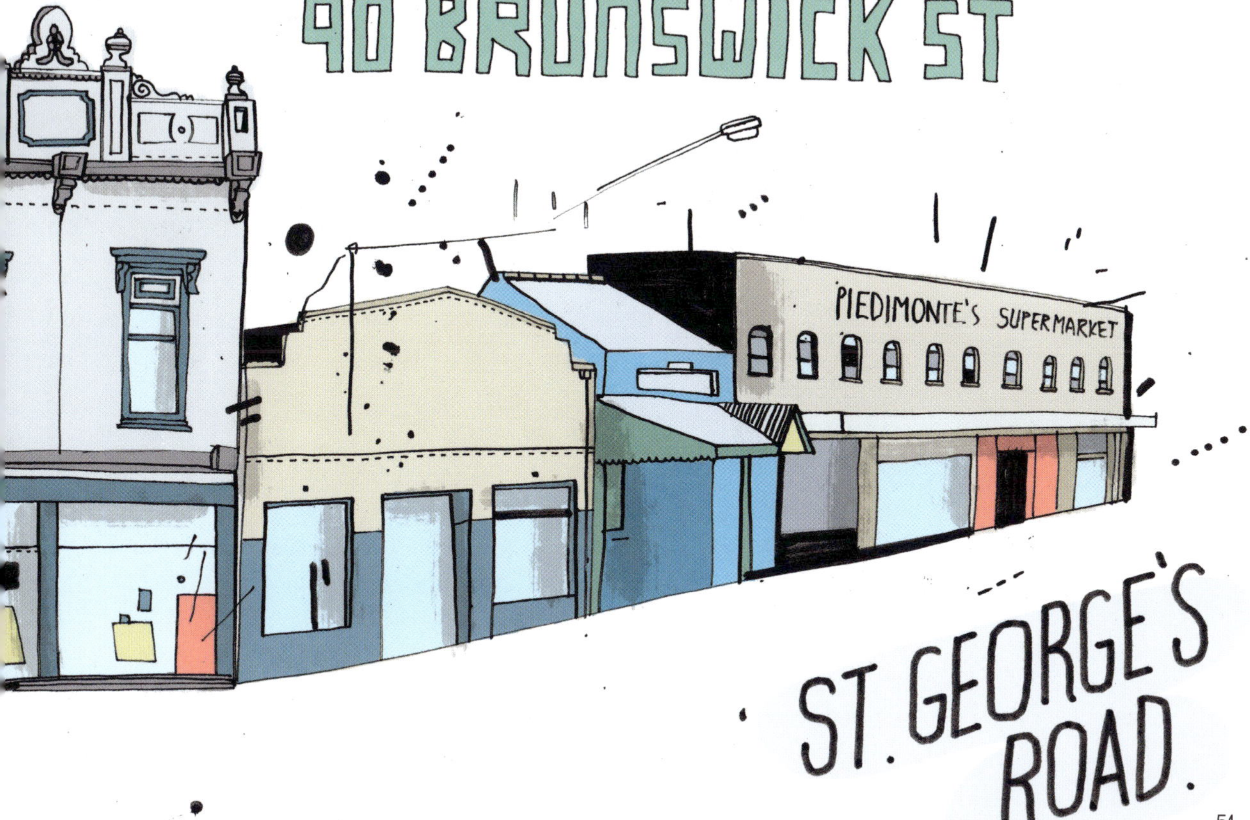

ST. GEORGE'S ROAD.

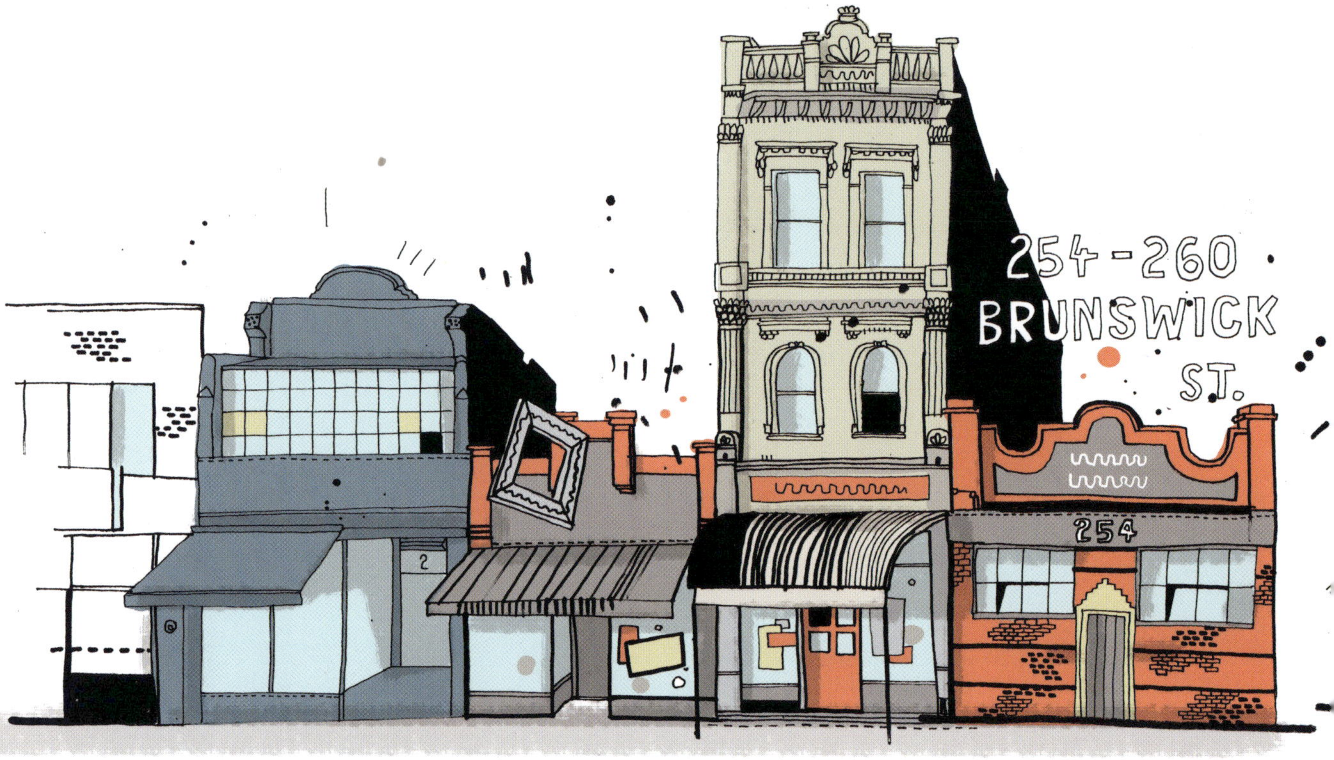
254-260
BRUNSWICK
ST.
254
2

CARLTON

MELBOURNE MUSEUM

DESIGNED BY DENTON CORKER MARSHALL ARCHITECTS

FINISHED IN 2001

THE LARGEST MUSEUM IN THE SOUTHERN HEMISPHERE.

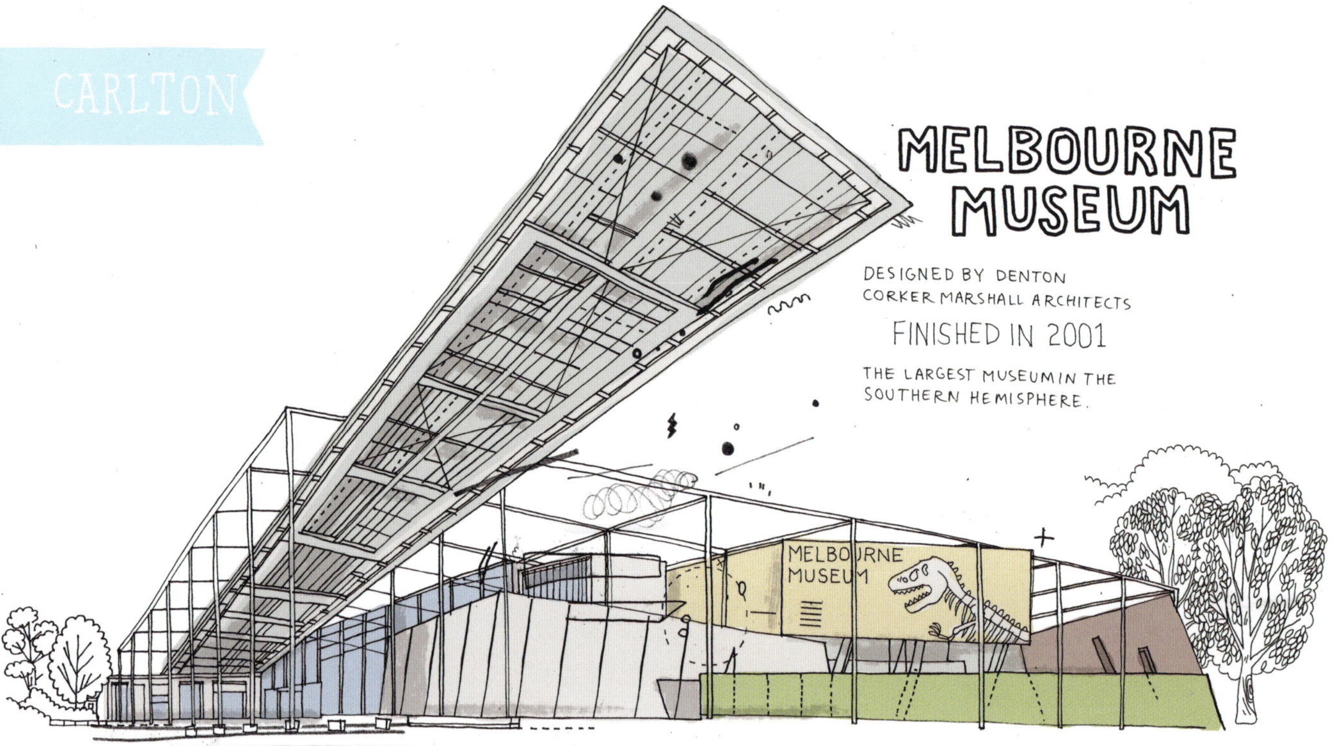
MELBOURNE
MUSEUM

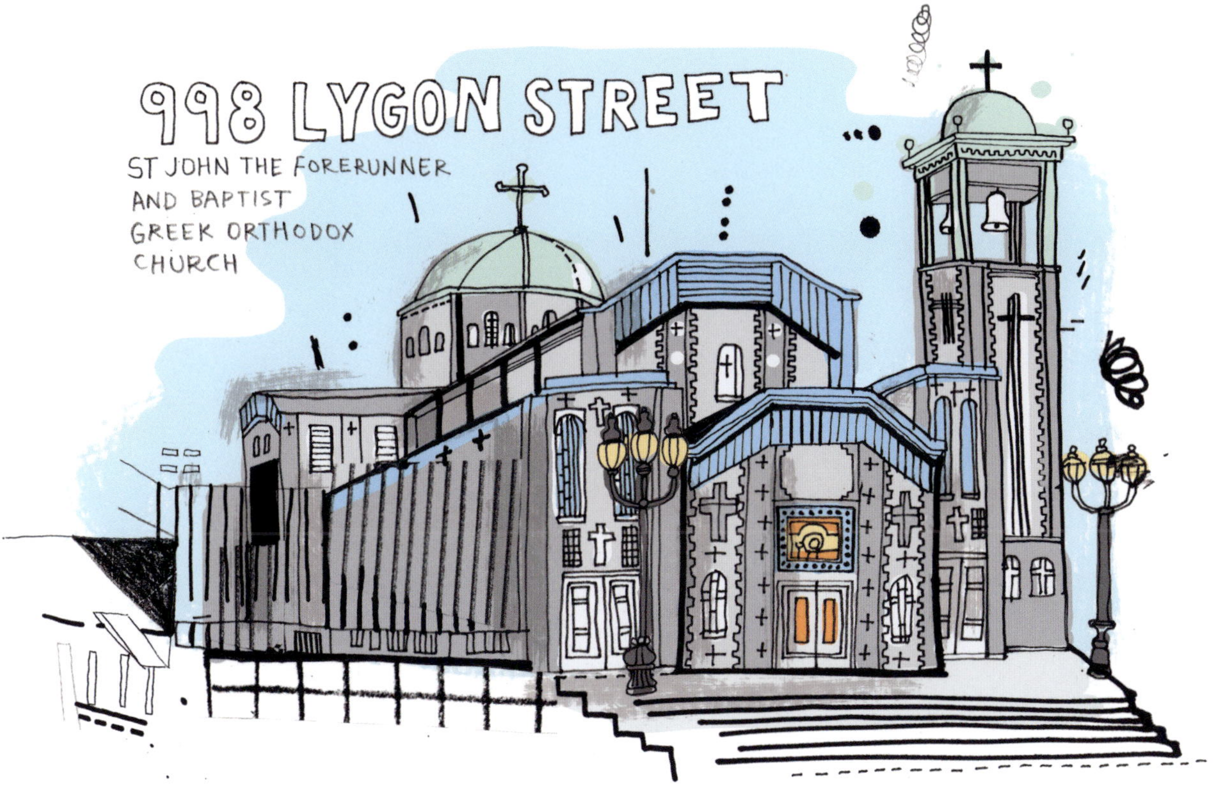
998 LYGON STREET
ST JOHN THE FORERUNNER
AND BAPTIST
GREEK ORTHODOX
CHURCH

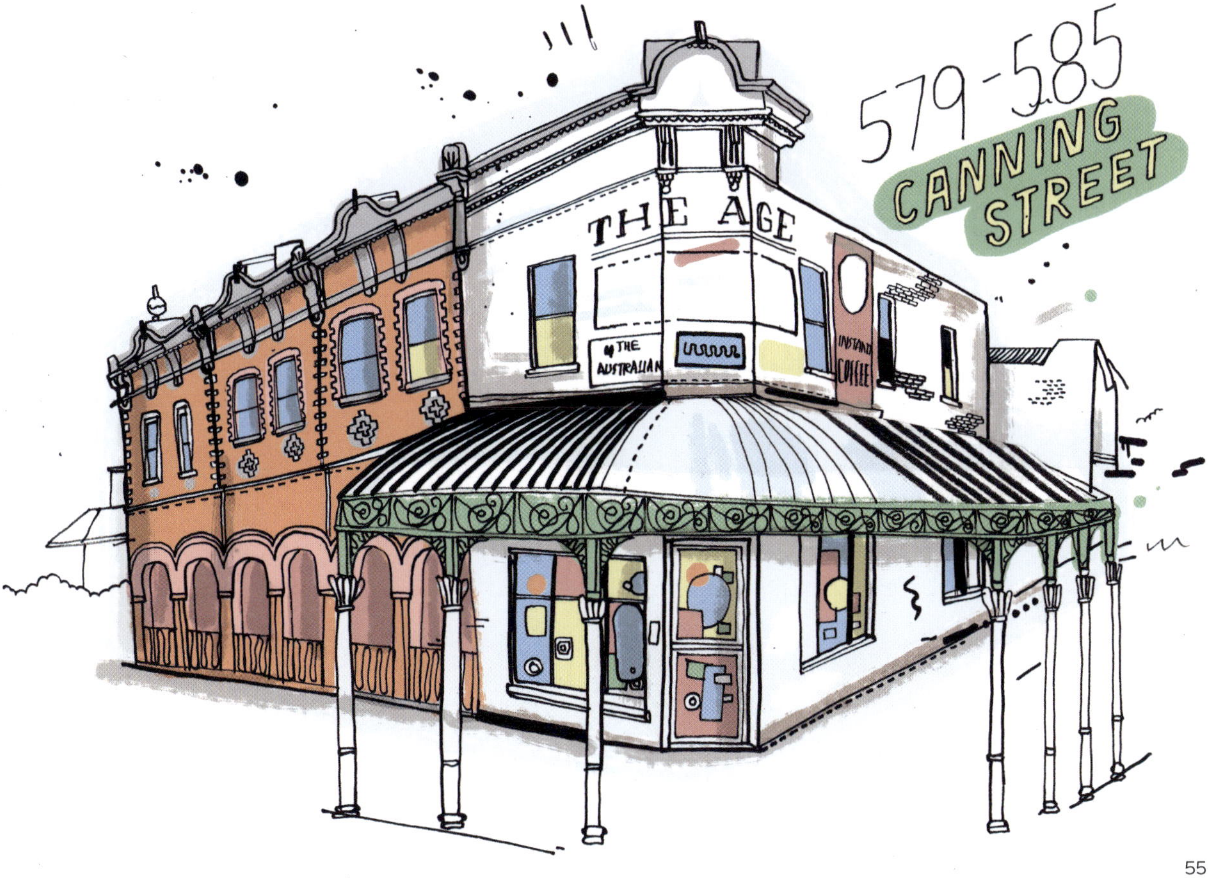
579-585
CANNING
STREET
THE AGE
THE AUSTRALIAN
INSTANT
COFFEE

PARKVILLE

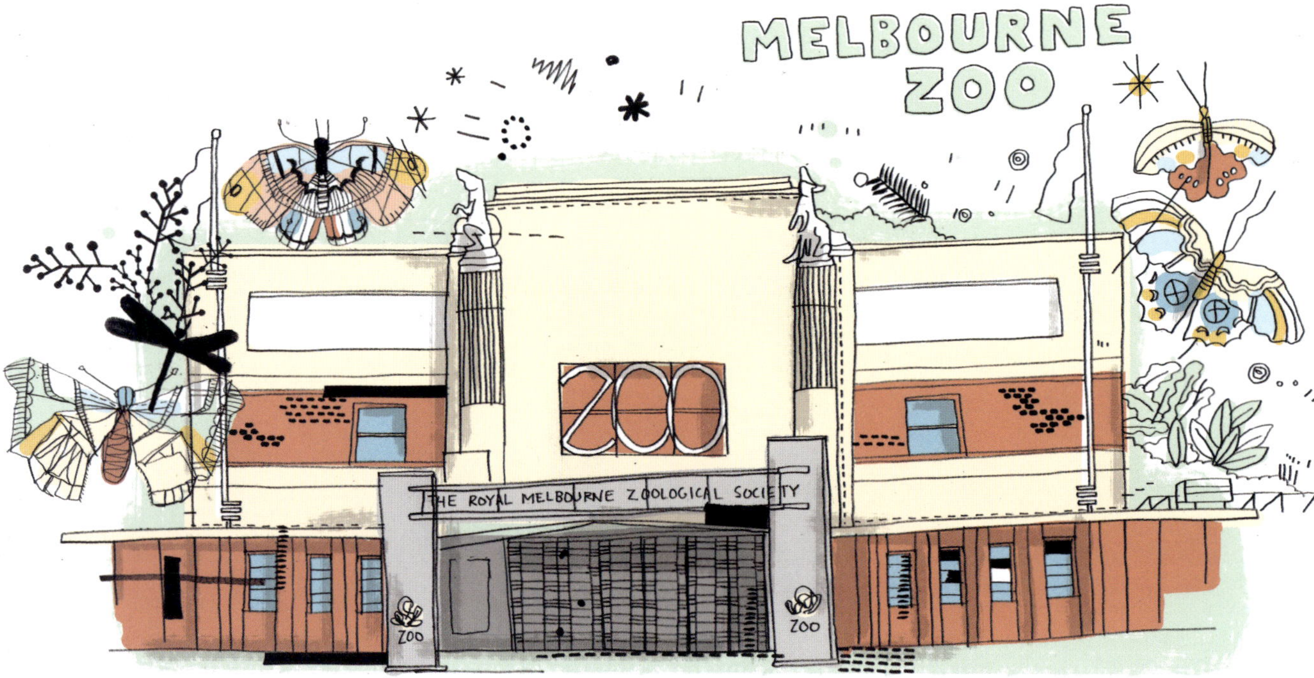
MELBOURNE ZOO
ZOO
THE ROYAL MELBOURNE ZOOLOGICAL SOCIETY
ZOO
ZOO

BRUNSWICK

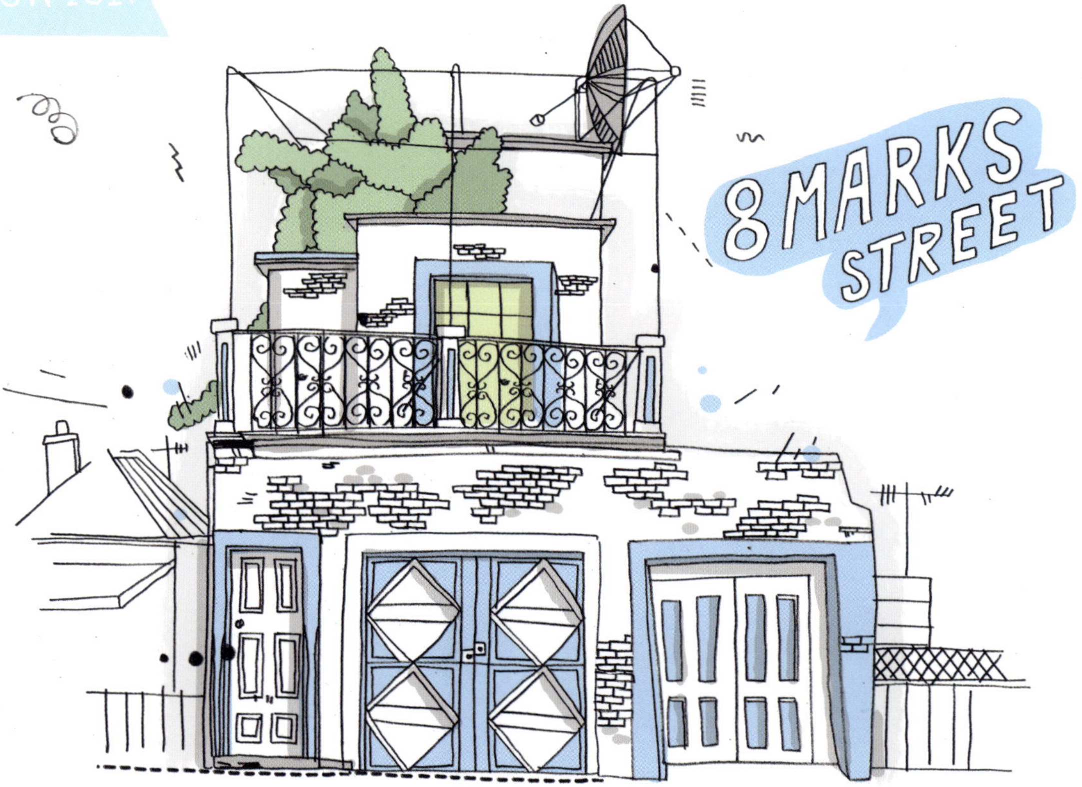
8 MARKS STREET

41 SUTHERLAND ST

H.M. PENTRIDGE PRISON
CHAMP ST. COBURG

COBURG

NED KELLY'S REMAINS WERE ONCE BURIED HERE

BUILT IN 1850

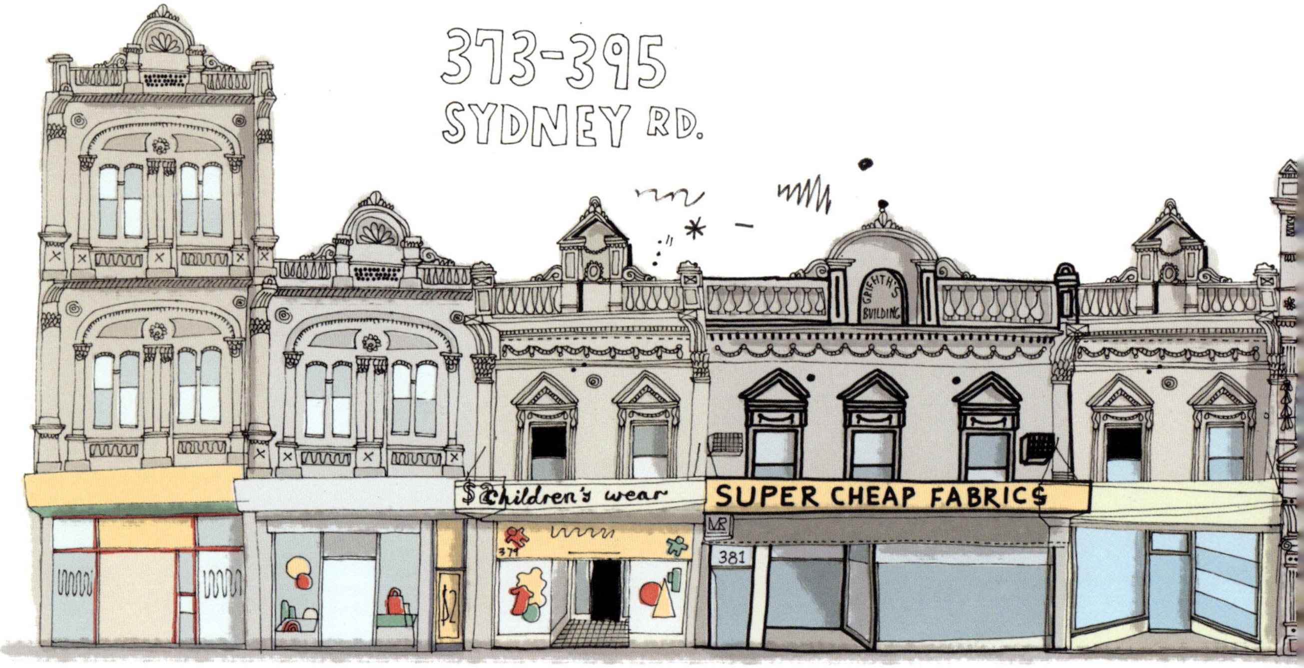

373-395 SYDNEY RD.

children's wear   SUPER CHEAP FABRIC$

ESSENDON

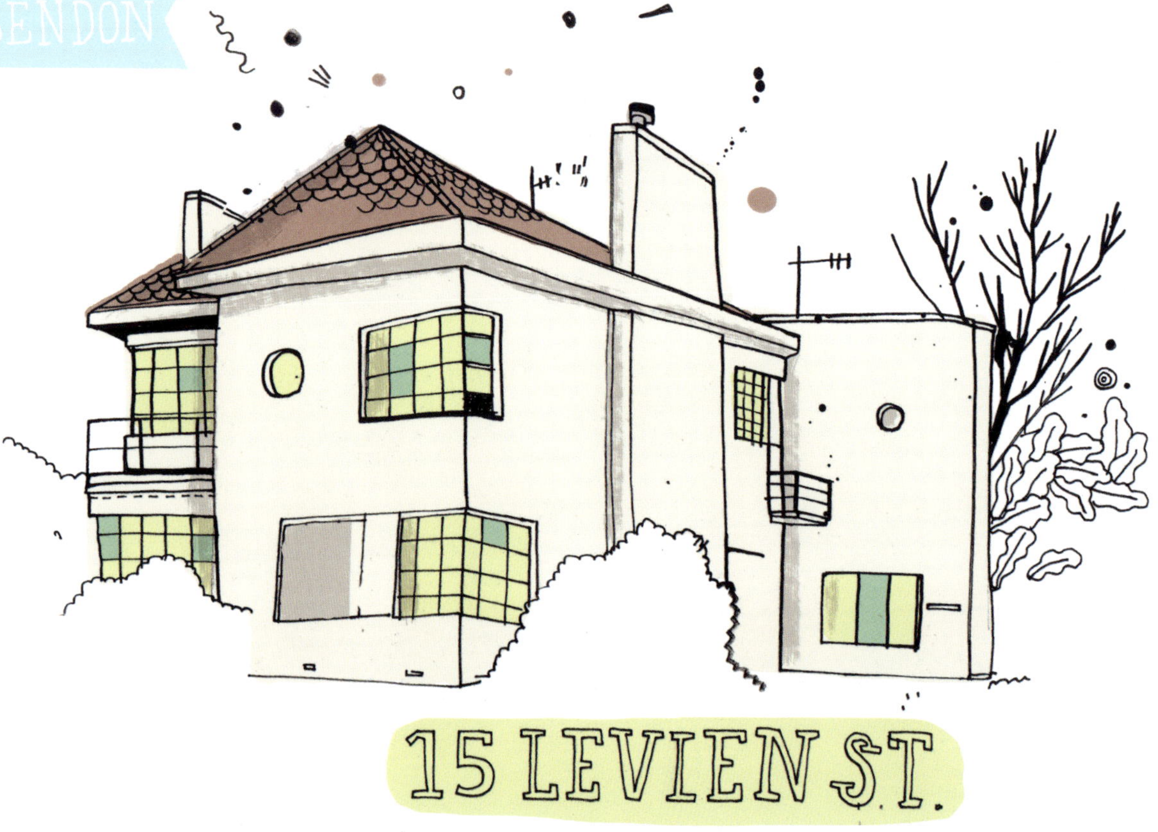

15 LEVIEN ST.

MOONEE PONDS

63 ARDMILLAN RD

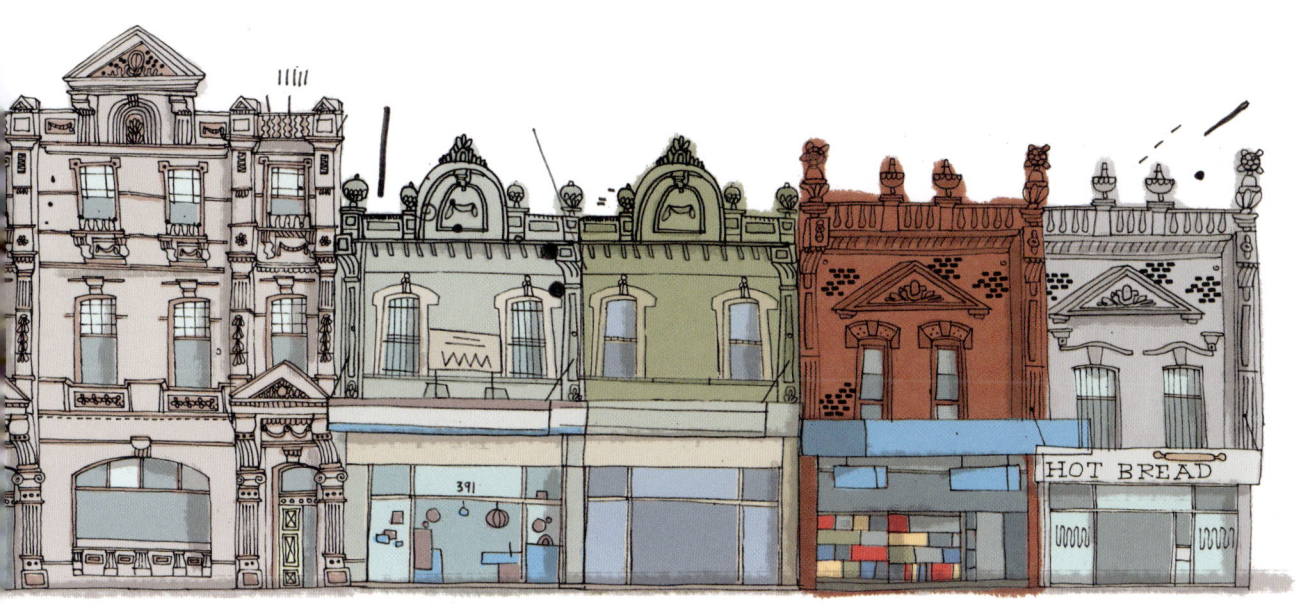

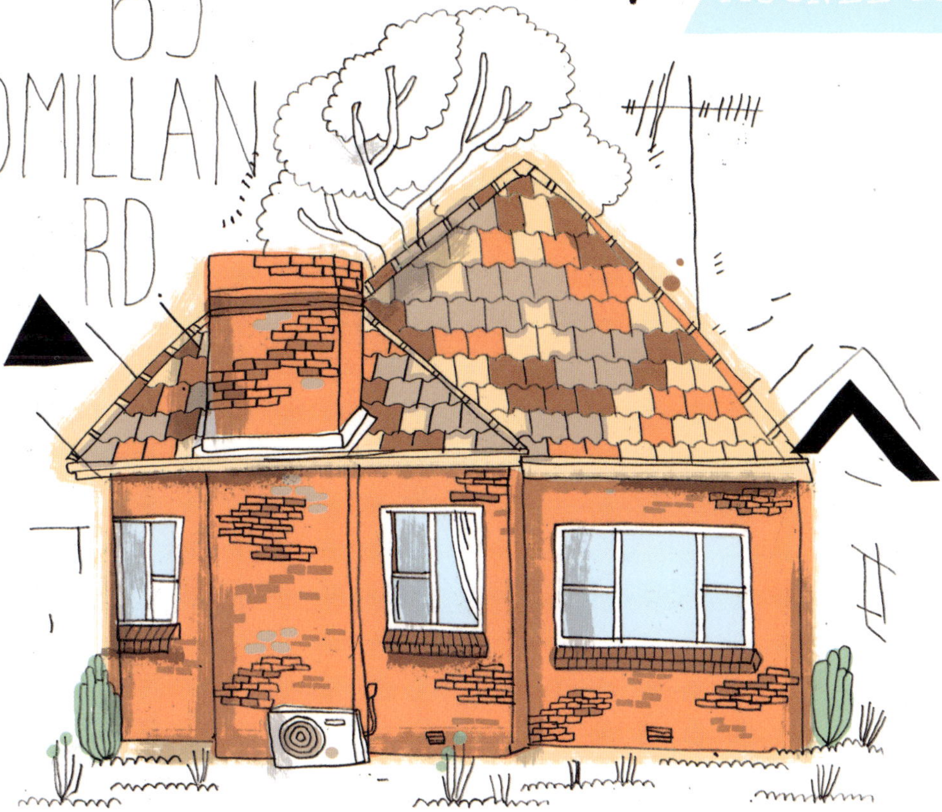

YARRAVILLE

8 BALLARAT STREET

37-39 HYDE ST

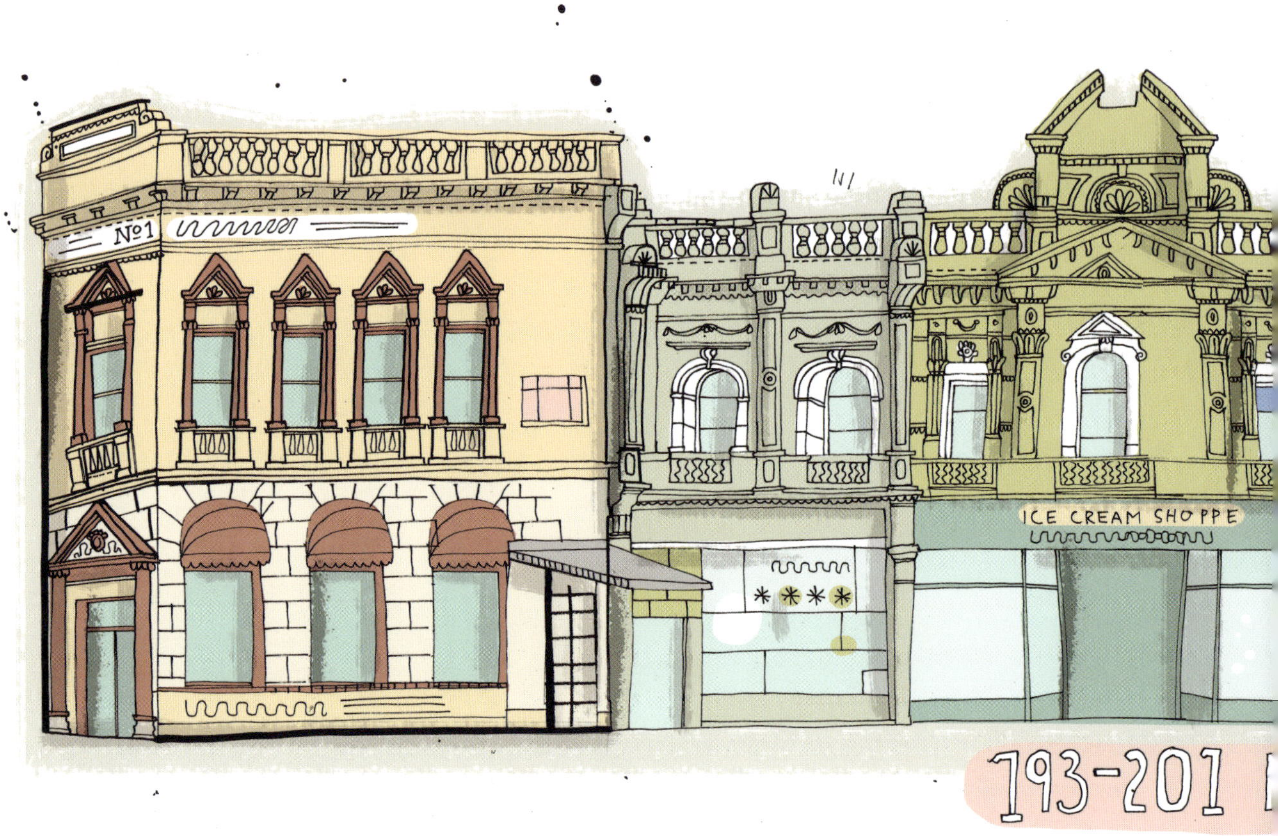
No1
ICE CREAM SHOPPE
193-201

SPOTSWOOD

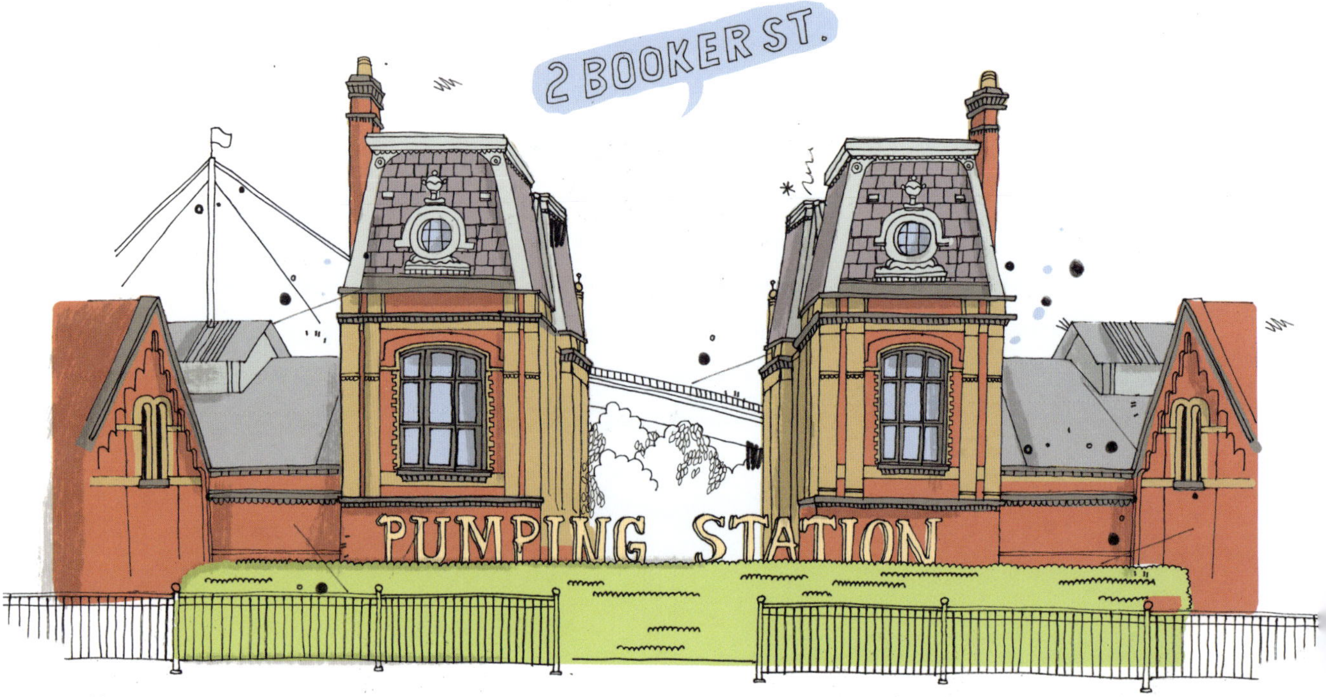
2 BOOKER ST.
PUMPING STATION

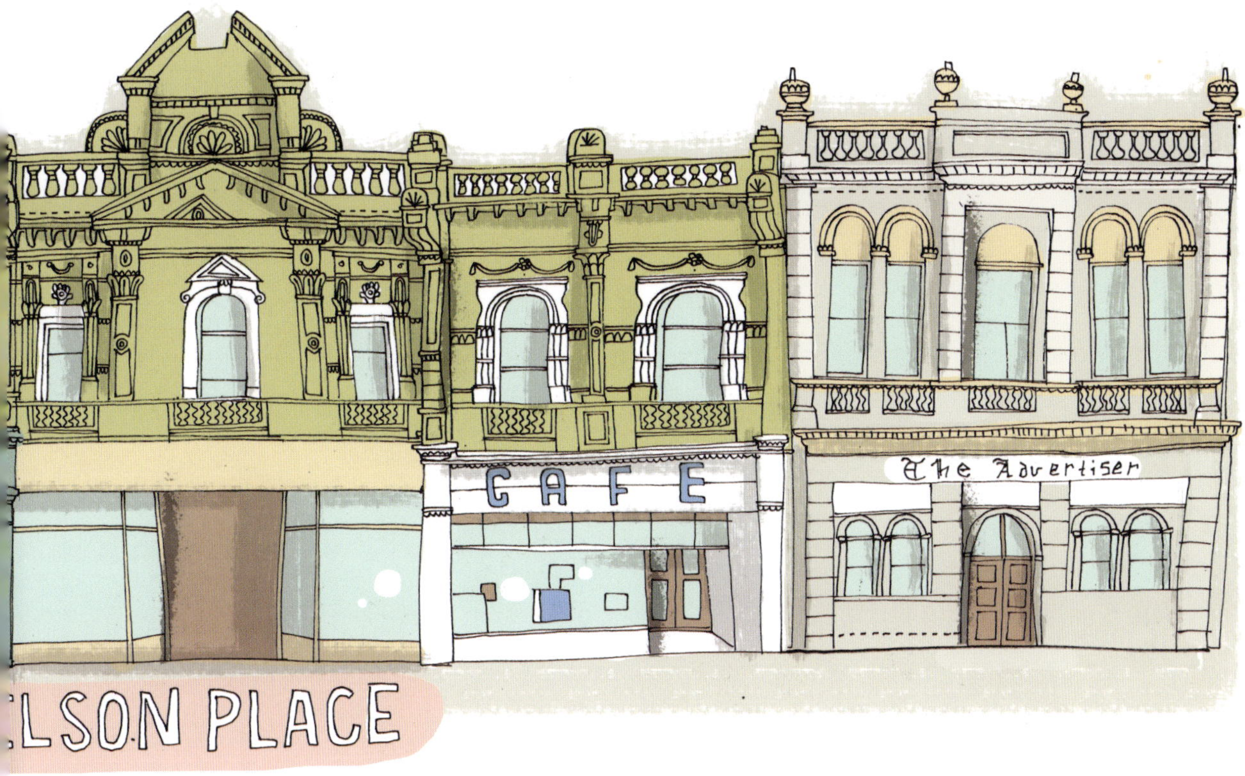
CAFE
The Advertiser
ELSON PLACE

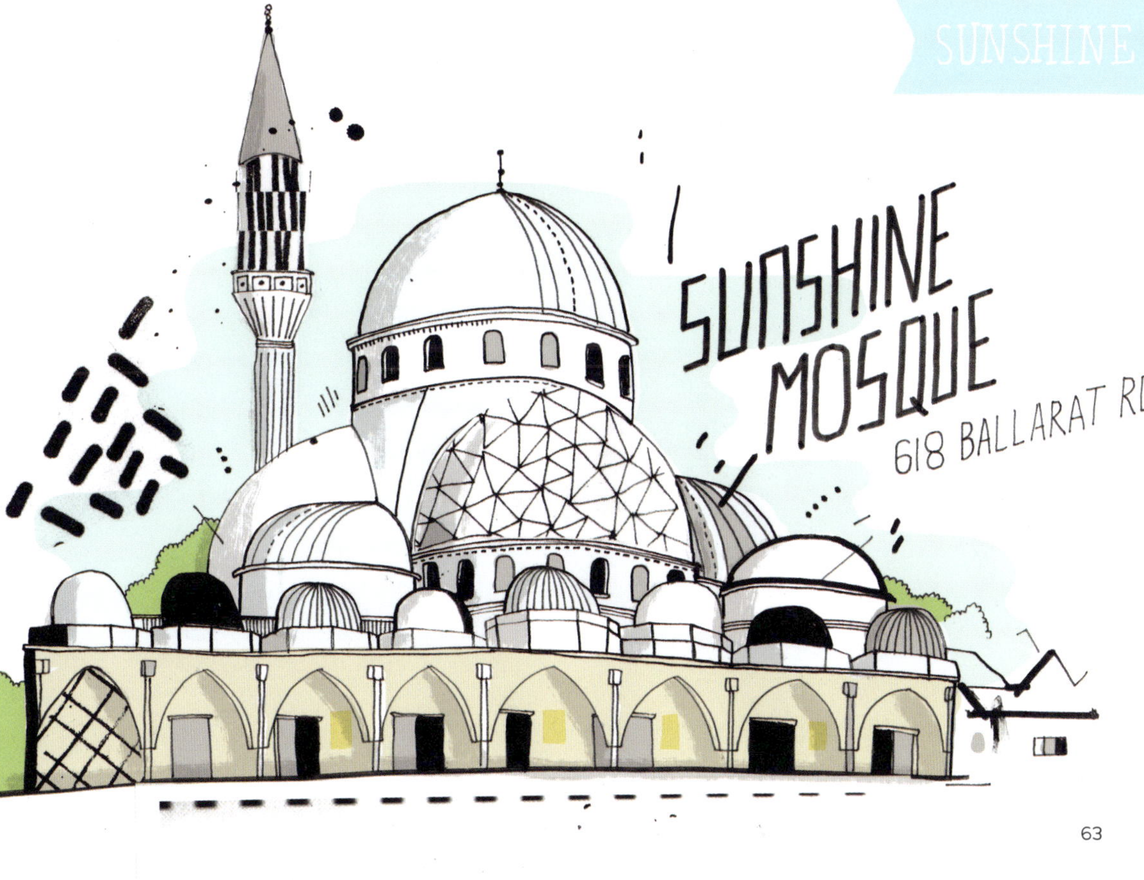
SUNSHINE
SUNSHINE MOSQUE
618 BALLARAT RD.

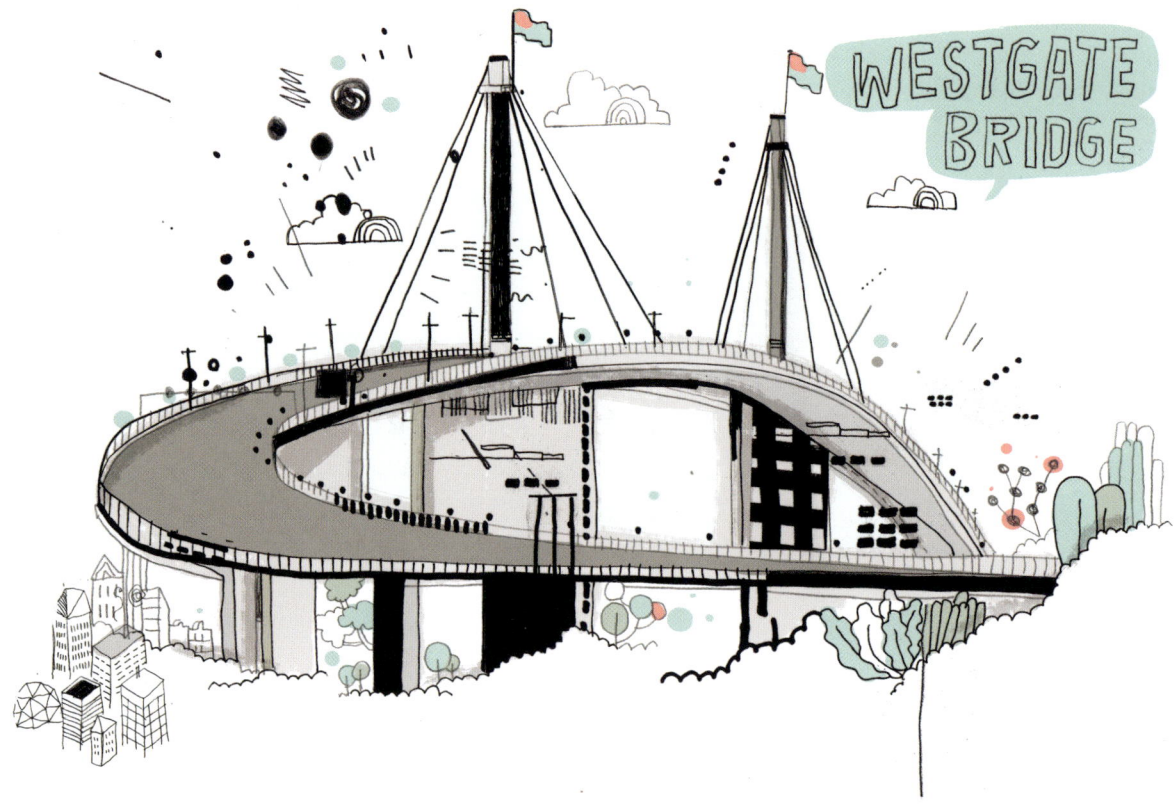

Thanks to everyone who ever took my hand and showed me around Melbourne, especially The Jacky Winter Group, my friends at Hardie Grant, James Harvey, Chloe and Adam, Marcus Westbury and his Facebook pals, Sass Cocker, Rosso, Missy, Fionna Fernandes, and my family.

Published in 2016 by Hardie Grant Books

Ground Floor, Building 1 • 658 Church Street, Richmond • Victoria, 3121 • www.hardiegrant.com.au
5th & 6th Floors • 52–54 Southwark Street • London SE1 1UN • www.hardiegrant.co.uk

All rights reserved. No part of this publication may be reproduced, stored in a retrieval system or transmitted in any form by any means, electronic, mechanical, photocopying, recording or otherwise, without the prior written permission of the publishers and copyright holders.

The moral rights of the author have been asserted.

Copyright text and illustrations © James Gulliver Hancock 2016

A Cataloguing-in-Publication entry is available from the catalogue of the National Library of Australia at www.nla.gov.au

All the Buildings in Melbourne
ISBN 978 1 74379 193 6

Publishing Director: Jane Willson
Designer and Illustrator: James Gulliver Hancock
Editor: Rihana Ries
Design Manager: Mark Campbell
Production Manager: Todd Rechner

Colour reproduction by Splitting Image Colour Studio
Printed in China by 1010 Printing International Limited